believing in yourself

Erik Blumenthal Dip. Psych. is a practising psychotherapist and analyst and Honorary President of the Swiss Society for Individual Psychology. He has written a number of books on child-rearing, self-education, marriage and old age, and is married with six children.

BY THE SAME AUTHOR

Peace with Your Partner: A Practical Guide to Happy Marriage,
ISBN 1–85168–136–1

To Understand and Be Understood: A Practical Guide to Successful Relationships, ISBN 1–85168–137–X

The Way to Inner Freedom: A Practical Guide to Personal Development, ISBN 1–85168–138–8

RELATED TITLES PUBLISHED BY ONEWORLD

Creating a Successful Family, Khalil Khavari and Sue Khavari,
ISBN 1–85168–008–X

Stress: An Owner's Manual, Arthur Rowshan,
ISBN 1–85168–140–X

Telling Tales: How to Use Stories to Help Your Children Deal with the Challenges of Life, Arthur Rowshan, ISBN 1–85168–139–6

Together Forever: A Handbook for Creating a Successful Marriage,
Khalil Khavari and Sue Khavari, ISBN 1–85168–061–6

Understanding Human Nature, Alfred Adler, ISBN
1–85168–021–7

Understanding Life: An Introduction to the Psychology of Alfred Adler, Alfred Adler, ISBN 1–85168–128–0

What Life Could Mean to You, Alfred Adler, ISBN
1–85168–022–5

believing in yourself

A Practical Guide to Building Self-Confidence

Erik Blumenthal

ONEWORLD

OXFORD

BELIEVING IN YOURSELF

Oneworld Publications
(Sales and Editorial)
185 Banbury Road
Oxford OX2 7AR
England

Oneworld Publications
(US Marketing Office)
PO Box 830, 21 Broadway
Rockport, MA 01966
USA

ISBN 1–85168–135-3

Cover design by Peter Maguire
Printed and bound by WSOY, Finland

contents

introduction

what does it mean to 'believe in yourself'?

Asked this question, most people would reply, 'being self-confident', and this is indeed the easiest aspect of self-belief to understand. But many people understand self-confidence as only referring to confidence in the face of difficult situations, or in situations of conflict. But belief in oneself means far more than this – 'I believe in myself' means not only that I am self-confident, but also that I am convinced of my own worth, of my ability to do something useful and to offer my talents to others. 'I believe in my husband/wife' means that I trust him/her and that I can always rely on him/her and that he/she will not deceive me. 'I believe in my children' means that I am convinced that they will make something of their lives, that I can learn from them and they from me, and that there is no reason to be afraid that they might not be able to cope with life. 'I believe in life and in the future' means that I anticipate the best will happen for human society and that we have a sustainable future.

Sarah gets up feeling positive about what the day has in store. Her husband, Matthew, is far slower at getting up and complains that he has slept badly. As usual, he knows exactly when and for how long he has lain awake. As they sit down to breakfast, Matthew carries on moaning, trying to involve Sarah in his complaints. But rather than be upset by his provocation, Sarah's positive mood is unaffected, as she knows Matthew's irritability has nothing to do with her. She has the self-belief not to let him get her down, and she proceeds with her tasks cheerfully.

Believing in yourself means acknowledging your own uniqueness. After all, despite the common features shared with others, every single human being is absolutely unique, and that includes you. Neither you, me, nor anyone else has existed at any time in the past, nor will we live again in the future. This in itself is proof of our importance as individuals, but is reaffirmed by the significance we all have for our contemporaries. There are very few of us who are not loved or valued by at least one person – our partner, mother, father, friend or colleague. In the final analysis, the advancement and decline of the entire world depends on the individual, as was realized by Confucius two and a half thousand years ago.

Every individual is responsible for the advancement and decline of the entire world.

Confucius

Most of you reading this book will be doing so because you feel you lack self-belief – you don't believe in your own abilities and undervalue yourself generally. People who have too little faith in themselves often admire others who radiate a great deal of self-confidence, or who merely put on a show of it. Such 'false' self-confidence often develops when people are convinced, deep down, of their own inadequacy – they show off because they need to. In order to veil their lack of genuine inner self-confidence they put on the appearance of being self-assured and are often successful in deceiving others. But if individuals do not believe in themselves, their ever-diminishing sense of self-importance may become almost infectious, and other people will start forming the same opinion. This downward spiral of discouragement means that individuals make life difficult both for themselves and for those around them.

But it is also possible to have an excess of self-belief. We all know people like this – we would normally describe them as arrogant. They are people whose confidence and self-assurance is out of proportion with the merits we feel they have. Both exaggeration and under-valuation are unhealthy. Exaggeration of the importance of the individual may lead to self-love, as illustrated in the fable of the peacock and peahen. The peacock and peahen are getting married. During the wedding ceremony the registrar asks why the magnificent peacock wishes to marry the plain-looking peahen, and the peacock replies, 'My bride and I are madly in love with me.'

Individuals who learn to believe more in themselves can also learn to believe more in the future. Every individual possesses undreamt-of abilities and powers, and self-belief can open the door to these, enabling the individual to become more free, independent and self-confident. The more I believe in myself and my powers, the more I can imagine progress in my life and in my relationships with others, the more I will encourage myself to work towards the things I aspire to, rather than believing they are beyond by reach. And not only can I consciously take my own fate into my hands, playing an active part in determining my personal future, but I can also contribute to creating a better, more positive, future for society.

This book is primarily concerned with helping you to come to terms with and accept who you are, so that you can strengthen your sense of self-worth and self-confidence. It explores both the practical self-development skills you can apply, involving making conscious decisions about how you behave, particularly in relation to others, and about how to deal with situations of conflict, and the spiritual faculties you can call upon, arguably the more effective instruments at our disposal for bringing about positive development. To use an analogy from medicine, if the practical measures we take tackle the symptoms of our lack of self-belief, working on the spiritual side of our natures targets the root cause. By developing the core of our inner being, we will become more able to be outwardly confident and self-assured. This will lead to a new quality of life, new experiences in our relations with other people, with ourselves, with material things and with the world. What has so far been perceived as life is only a poor imitation of life as it could be, i.e. a life with less prejudice and conflict, with less misfortune and suffering, a life full of joy, love, happiness and peace. Instead of being a mere fleeting sensation, happiness would then be a feeling of much greater intensity and duration.

The main point is to remain realistic, continually assessing and reassessing what is feasible. Although it is right not to allow oneself to be determined by others, it is often helpful in personal development to involve people close to you. Although your partner may at first appear to be the most suitable candidate for this, it is sometimes difficult for someone who is that emotionally involved with you to give you the objective help that is most effective. If necessary, you could consider consulting a psychotherapist, counsellor or religious leader, but remember that the main aim is to improve *your* self-belief, so make sure this remains the subject of discussion.

a brief introduction to Adlerian psychology

The practical, easy-to-learn techniques described in this book are based chiefly on the discoveries of Alfred Adler's school of Individual Psychology. Adler, an Austrian psychologist, is regarded as one of the founding fathers of modern psychoanalysis, along with Freud and Jung. He was a key member of Freud's circle in turn-of-the-century Vienna, although is perhaps best known for his controversial break with Freud over the causes of neurosis. The theories he introduced have made a significant contribution to contemporary psychology, with many of them, such as 'inferiority complex' and 'superiority complex', having entered everyday language without people knowing their source.

Central to Adlerian thought is the realization that individuals are social beings. Hundreds, if not thousands, of people contribute, albeit unconsciously, to the development and growth of any individual, and individuals are nothing without social relationships. Thus one of the key precepts of Individual Psychology is *social interest*, also known as *social awareness* or *feeling*. It refers to our active sense of belonging to a group or community, our feeling of connectedness to the rest of humanity which we must put into action if we are to contribute fully to society. The level of social interest individuals have dictates their ability to function effectively. Allied to social interest, the *social equality* of people who make up the human community is also a major principle of Individual Psychology. Differences between individuals, due to race, sex, age, education, status, ability, or other qualities, are artificial divisions – all individuals have equal value.

However significant the role of community may be in our development, each individual is unique, with his or her own unique contribution to make to society. Adler compared human beings to leaves – just as you cannot find two leaves of a tree that are identical, you cannot find two humans who are absolutely alike. We all have our own unique *life style*, a self-styled pattern for life that motivates our behaviour. We map out this life style in early childhood, based on the stimuli and experiences we have of the outside world, which, as small children, we can all too easily misinterpret. Therefore the key to understanding our life pattern is examining the impressions made on us at that time. Consequently, childhood memories, upbringing and the role of an individual in the family, particularly birth order, are central to Individual Psychology.

Although the past is important in establishing an individual's life style, Individual Psychology is primarily concerned with the present and future, with questions of meaning and purpose rather than causes. After all, the past cannot be changed; it can only be used to help us determine our futures. Another key precept is that we are all *goal-oriented* beings – all of our behaviour is motivated by goals we have set ourselves, more often than not unconsciously. Our long-term goals are motivated by our life style and reflect our perception of what we believe is best for us; our immediate goals are used to help us alter undesirable behaviour in the short-term. So, by exploring our behaviour – our thoughts, feelings and actions – we can identify the goals behind them, and begin to understand why we do what we do. Furthermore, Adlerian psychology holds that, in addition to being goal-oriented, we are *decision-making* beings, with the freedom to be responsible for nearly everything we do. So once we understand the motivation behind our behaviour, we can use our free creative power, our capacity for conscious action, to assess our goals and behaviour, and decide whether to change them into goals that can forge the positive future we want for ourselves.

As this demonstrates, conscious and unconscious

thoughts and deeds are central to Adlerian psychology. Unlike other schools of psychology, Adler did not believe that the conscious and unconscious were always in opposition, but often worked together towards the same goal. Examining childhood memories, for example, enables us to explore our conscious selves; dreams are key to an exploration of our unconscious being. They too are dominated by our goals, and can be what Adler described as 'an emotional rehearsal' of plans and attitudes for our waking behaviour, so examining them can help us understand ourselves.

Closely connected with goals and purpose is the Adlerian concept of *inferiority*. This has its roots in childhood – everyone starts life small and weak in a world of grown-ups, so from an early age we strive for self-improvement. Through love, courage and encouragement, many of us counter this inferiority and make the most of our abilities in what Adler called the 'useful side of life'. But many people also doubt their human value in adulthood, feeling that in some if not all aspects of their lives, they are not as good as others. But as people are social beings and do not wish others to share their view about their feelings of inferiority, they try to cover up by striving for some form of superiority. Indeed, striving for superiority is central to many of our goals. We try to move from what Adler described as a 'felt minus' to a 'desired plus', from a feeling of not being good enough to a belief that we are better than others. Strongly connected with this is the Adlerian concept of the *masculine protest*, a reaction by either sex to the prejudices of our society about masculinity and femininity. A man's behaviour may constitute a protest against the demands made on him by the myths of male superiority; a woman's may be a protest against the social limitations placed on women.

Adler's Individual Psychology also differs from other schools of psychology in that it considers the individual as a totality, as an indivisible whole, a *unity*, in which all the levels into which one might divide a human being – the animal, the human, and the spiritual – play a part. Each of these levels has its own laws, but they are interdependent, with many aspects of our behaviour drawing on all three. Exploring our psychology involves taking into account all three of these aspects, as each plays a vital part in determining what makes us who we are.

This is only a brief introduction to the key points of Adler's Individual Psychology, but does demonstrate its great strengths of simplicity and relevance. It is a very positive psychology, easy to understand with few new, scientific words. It is also easy to apply to one's own personal development, empowering the individual to exert more control over his or her present and future.

---

individual psychology and the individual

Every human being is

- a unique individual
- a social being
- the equal of every other human being
- goal-directed
- decision-making
- responsible
- a unity of body, soul and spirit

These are characteristics of every human being, irrespective of where he or she lives on the earth. We could call this the 'skeleton' of the human soul. Just as every person is physically made up of a head, two arms and legs and a skeleton, these are the elements that make up the souls of all members of the human race.

What really makes Adler's work relevant today is the importance of social feeling. In our age of individualism, Individual Psychology seeks to help individuals develop themselves into more effective members of the community and thus to promote the development of the community as a whole.

author's note

As a practising therapist, Individual Psychology appeals to me because it seems more realistic and practical than other schools of psychology, particularly because of its goal-directedness. Asking the question 'why?' about something you do, or some other aspect of your behaviour, only directs you to the past, which you cannot change. But asking 'what for?' – for what purpose did I do this or think that? – leads us far deeper into our selves and our attitudes, and may give us information on which we can act to cause conscious change.

During the many years that I have worked as a psychotherapist and counsellor, I have developed, as most psychotherapists do, some of my own techniques. Three in particular are a development from the ideas of Alfred Adler, and as they feature quite prominently in both this and my other books, I should go through them briefly here.

As well as the incredible power we have of making decisions (most of them unconsciously) about what to think, feel, say and do, I stress another even bigger asset we can use more consciously, namely *the power of believing*. Before now, believing had two meanings; first, in a religious context, referring to faith in the existence of a divine being or beings; second, in the sense of 'assume' or 'suppose'. But there is a third meaning, referring to our inner belief, our inner spiritual power. This is a uniquely human power that we use from morning to night, but of which we are rarely conscious. Medical doctors know of this power, for example when they experiment with placebos, but it remains underestimated as a major force in our psychological make-up.

The second important point is *spirituality*. Asking people what they understand by the word 'spiritual' produces predictable answers: 'the opposite of materialistic', or 'it means to be free from the limitations of space and time'. But these do not give us the real answer. If we ask, 'What is the opposite of spirituality?', we get a better idea – the answer is 'egocentredness'. So spiritualization is the path from egocentredness to spirituality. Spiritualization is one of the most important tasks of our time; theoretically very simple, but practically the most urgent and most difficult task we have.

For religious people, spirituality is uniquely allied to their belief in 'God', but there is a spiritual dimension to all of us. Alexander Müller, a student of Adler and a tutor of mine, defines religion as 'the relation of human beings with God *and* with human beings. This last point is key to understanding how people in distress or who are not at ease with certain aspects of their lives can be helped. First, there is psychotherapeutic support from the major schools of psychology, all of which have approaches that can help. Or you can help yourself either using a book such as this one, or with the help of a person who can assist you by virtue of the mutual understanding, respect, trust and love that exist between you. But you should not discount prayer, meditation and contemplation in helping you to deal with problems in your life. Prayer and contemplation put us in touch with our sense of spirituality and contribute to the growth of our spiritual faculties and skills, particularly our insight and understanding, which are very important in maintaining our self-confidence and ability to deal with the challenges of life.

part one

Guiding Principles

In the Introduction we established the importance of the individual and looked at the general features of Alfred Adler's school of Individual Psychology. In the following chapters we will concentrate on the general principles you need in order to develop your self-belief. In particular, this involves looking at two aspects of yourself and your behaviour: the psychological and the spiritual.

1 a psychological view of human nature

The key psychological principles initiated by Alfred Adler that were raised in the Introduction can be helpfully summarized as follows:

- optimism
- goal identification
- purpose
- encouragement
- belonging
- use of the past
- a holistic view

I shall go through these key points one by one.

optimism rather than pessimism

It is not difficult to see that pessimists are programmed for failure. As they see the worst in things, they perceive little harm in opening their mouths when it would be better to keep their silence and keeping their mouths shut when it would be right to speak up. Although they seem to see nothing but the negative in both themselves, others and situations, pessimists have a secret sense of superiority, priding themselves on the fact that they foresee failure. If they are unexpectedly successful they say to themselves, 'Something must have gone wrong!'. And they are right. So their attitude will not change, even though they are the ones to suffer most as a result of their outlook.

If we compare optimists with pessimists, we realize almost instantly that optimism is a more useful attitude to life. Optimists are more likely to be successful because they believe success is achievable and do not give failure a chance. If optimists unexpectedly fail, they are not discouraged but are convinced that they will have better luck next time. They will say to themselves, 'The sun doesn't shine every day and there will always be times when other people or circumstances are more powerful than me. Let's make sure I do better in a similar situation next time.' And they probably will be successful once again when the next time comes along. What optimists may not be conscious of is the fact that they contribute to their success simply by virtue of having the right attitude, and are thus able to cope with each particular situation. In other words, optimists use their powers realistically and sensibly, tailoring their actions for success.

> *Nothing is too great or too good to be true. Do not believe that we can imagine things better than they are. In the long run, in the ultimate outlook, in the eye of the creator, the possibilities of existence, the possibilities open to us, are beyond our imagination.*
>
> Oliver Lodge

identifying our goals

Assessing character and behaviour from the point of view of the hidden goals behind them is an unusual way of viewing human nature requiring a change in our pattern of thinking. As discussed in the Introduction, we are used to asking the question 'why?' when faced with something we do not understand that evokes emotions like distress or anger. But asking the reason for thoughts, feelings or behaviour often does not bring the real problem to light. As far as our inner selves are concerned, it is much more helpful to ask about motivations and goals, rather than reasons or causes – the question 'for what purpose?' is far more useful.

short-term goals

As undesirable behaviour can more often than not be traced to one of only five, often unconscious, short-term goals, knowing about them can be extremely valuable. The person displaying the behaviour is usually seeking any one or a combination of the following:

1. an excuse for his or her own shortcomings (whether these are real or imagined)
2. care and attention
3. a sense of superiority or at least avoidance of inferiority
4. revenge
5. retreat

It is easy to attribute some physical or psychological justification to a physical weakness which has no evident cause, and these excuses will generally be accepted. But there are very few simple physical symptoms or behaviour patterns that cannot be attributed to at least one of these five immediate goals.

Here are some easy-to-recognize behaviour patterns. You might find it helpful to match these with the short-term goals we have listed – remember there may be more than one goal involved. You will find my interpretation in Appendix 1 starting on p. 127.

Karen is 21 and blushes whenever she is in the company of other people. This tends to make people feel sorry for her, and they try and make up for the feeling that they may have embarrassed her by going out of their way to talk to her and make her feel comfortable. So Karen very rarely finds herself alone, and normally has a lot of people with her.

A woman aged 34 suffers from back pain. This gives her an excellent excuse to pass on the burden of housework to her husband so that she has more time to pursue her interests.

James is 44 and is married to Anna, some twelve years his junior. Although he finds his wife very attractive, the physical side of their relationship has been suffering for the past few months as James always feels tired, but there seems to be no physical cause for his exhaustion. His young wife respects this, but is not happy about the situation and can't help feeling there is more to James' 'fatigue' than he is admitting.

Tom, a seventeen-year old, has started getting frequent headaches which prevent him from studying, with the result that his marks at school have dropped significantly. Tom's father is getting increasingly distressed about this, as he is keen that his son does the best that he can and achieves the things in life that he did not. He is particularly keen that Tom goes to university, as he really regrets not taking up the place he was offered, but Tom seems more interested in repairing his motorbike all hours of the day.

Now think about some of your behaviour patterns. Can you attribute these to any one or a combination of the immediate goals?

long-term goals

In addition to these immediate goals, as we discovered in the Introduction, there are also long-term goals. These are part of an individual's 'life style', and, just like the short-term goals, are pursued unconsciously. These long-term goals can vary markedly from one person to another.

There are four elements to the life style concept. The first is the small child's unconscious view of other people, which can range from friendly to hostile. In most cases, it is the mother who first takes care of the child, and so she is the first 'other person' with whom the child comes into contact. The second element is the child's view of itself. Does it see itself as 'weak' or 'strong', as 'big' or 'small'? The third element is the way in which the child judges life itself, ranging from 'pleasant' to 'unpleasant'. The fourth element is made up of the long-term goals the child unconsciously sets itself, which reflect how it should best react and behave in order to survive, and these persist into adulthood.

Here are some common long-term goals, in no particular order. You may find it helpful to go through and tick the ones that apply to you. You may not consider some of the goals listed particularly pleasant, and you may not want to admit to them, but it is important to be honest with yourself. Recognizing your goals will help you better understand your behaviour as you work to improve your self-belief.

☐   I want to know where I belong.
☐   I want to be praised.
☐   I want to be big and strong.
☐   I want to be the centre of attention.
☐   I want to be someone special.
☐   I want to be good.
☐   I want to please.
☐   I don't want to be told what to do.
☐   I want to show that I'm someone to be reckoned with.

- ☐ I have to be wary of other people.
- ☐ I must be careful about showing my feelings.
- ☐ I mustn't make any mistakes.
- ☐ I must have everything under control.
- ☐ I want to be intellectually superior.
- ☐ I won't let myself be put down.
- ☐ I want to be morally superior.
- ☐ I must get others to support me.
- ☐ I want to enjoy life.
- ☐ I want to make something of my life.
- ☐ I want to have an easy life.
- ☐ I can't rely on others.
- ☐ I want to achieve something.
- ☐ I have to stand up for myself.
- ☐ I mustn't reveal my incompetence.
- ☐ I want to be first.
- ☐ I want to show that I'm not just anybody.
- ☐ I want to be outstanding.
- ☐ I must get others to feel sorry for me.
- ☐ I must let others offend me so as to be able to look down on them.
- ☐ I must be right.
- ☐ I want to be rich.
- ☐ I want to be independent.
- ☐ I have to know everything.
- ☐ I always want to be just.
- ☐ I don't want others to think ill of me.
- ☐ I want security.
- ☐ I don't want to take risks.
- ☐ I want to understand everything.

☐   I am prepared to adapt.

☐   I will not let myself be drawn away from my chosen path.

☐   Life must be interesting.

☐   I want to help others.

☐   I want to be considered a good sport.

☐   I want to be loved by everybody.

☐   Others must admire me.

giving a purpose to life

Absence of self-belief can develop when our lives seem to have little purpose, when we do not know what we are working towards, even in the short term, let alone any further. Modern psychologists are increasingly realizing that one of the main difficulties individuals encounter is that they see too little purpose in life itself and particularly in their own lives. People search for purpose – whether consciously or unconsciously – but it is inevitable that they will not find it, because a purpose to our lives is not hidden somewhere waiting to be discovered. It is our responsibility, part of our life's work, to give purpose to our lives, to decide what our own purpose is, and then strive to achieve it.

Man forgets his purpose and thus he forgets who he is and what life means.

Francis Schaeffer

Although the purpose behind different individuals' lives will vary considerably, there are some general patterns that would seem to apply to us all, and are linked with our development through the various stages of human life. We could say that the purpose of our 'first life' is to develop the body during the nine months in the womb, the purpose being to prepare it for our 'second life' outside. The embryo develops eyes and ears, which it does not need in the womb but certainly will after birth. What then is the purpose of our 'second life'? For most of it, we will all have different purposes, linked to our perception of what constitutes achievement, what we consider of value and how ambitious we are. For those with a spiritual inclination, just as the embryo is being prepared for the world to come, we may feel that it is part of our purpose to prepare ourselves for whatever may follow.

Individual Psychology sees the purpose of life in the efforts individuals take to develop themselves into more effective members of the community and thus to promote the development of the community as a whole. When you start thinking about the purpose of your life, don't worry if you find it impossible to find a single answer. The mere process of searching will help you see the aspects of your life that trouble you on a daily basis in an entirely different way. Try and spend some time thinking about what you think the purpose of life is – it will help you put things into perspective.

perfection

Asking yourself about the purpose of your life will set you up well for the path to self-belief, but before you set out, you must also incorporate perfection into your life purpose. Although perfection is an eternally unachievable goal, it will give focus and direction to your efforts. Simply the desire to do the right thing can, in itself, propel us along the right path, and give us the encouragement and purpose we need to continue.

But you must remember that, because perfection is so far off, even unattainable, you cannot expect to get there overnight, all in one go. Aim to get as close as you can in small steps, with small, achievable goals every day, week, month or year.

There are certain souls who desire to arrive at perfection all at once, and this desire keeps them in constant disquiet.

Alphonsus Liguori

In striving for perfection, it is just as important to develop the courage to be imperfect. After all, to be human is to err. Wishing completely to avoid mistakes is not only unrealistic but also discouraging, because we cannot achieve it. What counts is to make a conscious effort to overcome our deficiencies, to turn major faults into minor ones. We will be dealing more with this later in this book.

For frail mortals, perfection is achieved not by never falling, but by rising every time we fall.

John O'Brien

the importance of encouragement

Self-belief and encouragement are intimately linked – believing in ourselves is a prerequisite for the self-encouragement that is absolutely essential in today's world. We have to face so many ups and downs in our modern lives, it is vital that we encourage ourselves to keep going, particularly when times are hard. Encouragement is one of the most important tasks facing us today, but to encourage ourselves, we must believe in ourselves – we must believe we are worth all this effort!

One of the highest of human duties is the duty of encouragement.

William Barclay

Encouragement is also of fundamental importance in our relationships with others. If we encourage another person,

21

we are emphasizing his or her positive aspects and expressing our honest appreciation. Encouraging others can be of help both to them and to us. Mutual encouragement between partners or friends can help both parties to increase the amount of happiness in their lives, to reshape their lives anew every day, to move towards perfection in small steps. Simply the desire to encourage, to do the right thing by ourselves or by our partner or friends, can, in itself, be encouraging.

Just as is the case with myself, I can only encourage another person if I believe in him or her. We live in a competitive age, in a society in which discouragement features all too prominently. We discourage ourselves, and have often done so since early childhood, perhaps feeling that we did not come up to the expectations of our parents or the achievements of our siblings. A person who is in a state of discouragement will take refuge in his or her ego, around which all thoughts and strivings revolve. He or she will be self-centred; this is not the same as egotism or selfishness, rather it is egocentricity, a state in which one's thoughts, actions and motivations revolve exclusively around oneself. Discouraged people have too little faith in themselves and compare themselves to others because of their fear of being inadequate or inferior. They continually ask themselves what impression they make on others, what others think of them, and whether others notice how incompetent and inadequate they are.

We often do not notice how it has become second nature for us to discourage others too. We often strive for the apparent advantage of achieving a sense of superiority over other people by means of condescension, criticism or reproach. At times, we discourage to perfection, although usually without being conscious of doing so. As discouragement is most damaging in early childhood, it is important that encouragement has now become a major principle in child-rearing. Despite this development, although many parents know about the importance of encouragement, they have no idea how to implement it with their children. They feel discouraged themselves and often believe only in what they expect or hope their children will be like. What is really important, however, is to have faith in children as they are, loving them as they are, with all their faults and weaknesses. It is important for parents not only to do the right things, but also to observe carefully how children react to their efforts, to ensure that it is true encouragement their children are receiving, rather than an expectation of what the parents want. Children have their own thoughts and feelings; they do not necessarily react in the way we expect.

the need to belong

That individuals are social beings with a need to belong was recognized as long ago as Aristotle, who stated that man is 'naturally a political animal'. The need to belong, to feel part of a community beyond oneself, even if only in relation to a single other person, is the eternal goal common to all individuals. It is the most significant goal for the life of an individual, however much he or she is, or is not, aware of it. Everyone wants to know where they belong and where their place in the world is. Even people that seek to be separate from the rest of the world still define their existence in relation to the larger community – it is just that whereas many people choose to live as *part* of that community, they seek to define themselves as *apart* from it.

While a certain degree of how we define ourselves comes from our community, either a small community or humanity at large, it is important that we do not attach values to different types of community, and remember that it is belonging to humanity rather than a smaller community that is most important. Attaching values to groups of people on the basis of sex, generation, race, nationality, income or education, is unjust.

Very often, loss of self-belief is linked with a feeling of not belonging, a feeling that one is somehow different to everyone else and therefore inferior and less valuable. It is easy to blame society at large for this, to say that society is not as tolerant as it should be of people that do not conform to some type of 'norm'. This may indeed be the case, but the important thing to remember is that we are important for ourselves, for our uniqueness. More often than not our feelings of not belonging are just a symptom of our insecurity and are not true at all, but even if we do feel 'different', working at our self-belief will help us value that difference as it should be valued, rather than allowing it to make us feel weak and inferior.

using the past to build the future

It is important to learn not to regard circumstances and causes as determining what happens in our lives. What determines our lives is us – to coin an old phrase, 'Life is what you make it.' By consciously applying what we have learned from the past, we can build a future determined only by us and achieve a sense of freedom.

To achieve this successfully, it may even be necessary to choose to forget, depending on the circumstances. The past has only two purposes – first to learn from it, then to forget it, to discard the unnecessary. But we must be very aware of our reasons for consciously forgetting an aspect of our past. There is a significant difference between my forgetting something for reasons of economy, because I simply do not need it, and my wanting to forget something because it seems to me to be awkward, unpleasant or inconvenient. No one likes to remember negative things unless remembrance of them promises to be advantageous in the present. We all prefer to forget something bad that we have done or a mistake we have made, more because we want to relieve ourselves of the burden of guilt associated with the deed rather than the deed itself. It is similarly difficult for us to forget a friend's bad behaviour towards us, however good the relationship might be. We will regularly use the memory of the behaviour to give ourselves a feeling of superiority over the friend in question.

The important thing is to put all our effort into acting in the present. It is fine to forget something after having learned from it. What is important is that what we do with the past is meaningful and constructive for the present and future. We should not worry about forgetting the mistake and putting the guilt to one side, as long as we have learned a lesson from the experience, and present and future action will be changed for the better. Similarly, the memory of a friend's bad behaviour has no place in the present as it is inspiring only negative behaviour in us. The best course of action would be consciously to eliminate it from our memory in order to eradicate the negative consequences it may have both for our relationship with our friend and for our view of ourselves.

As we shall see in the next chapter, memory is an extremely important 'inner sense', which, used consciously, can be a constructive and powerful tool in our path to self-belief.

taking a holistic view

As we discussed in the Introduction, the human individual is a single entity, a unit, a whole, but a unity of many different elements. This can be explained by the concept I describe as 'plane thinking'. At the same time as an individual is a single unit, he or she lives on various levels, or planes, of existence. The body, for instance, belongs to the mineral plane, with the main function being existence. The next plane is that of plant life. This adds further functions to those of the mineral plane – growth, reproduction and sensitivity. But most obvious in relation to the human body is the next level, the animal plane. The characteristic functions of the animal plane are, in the first place, the physical, chemical and biological functions of life, growth, movement and development. A further important function is perception, with the five outer senses of sight, hearing, smell, taste and touch. Other functions on this level are instincts, the ability to adapt and to learn, a certain memory capacity, and, in particular, reactions and emotions.

The next plane, that of the human soul, is unique to human individuals. Here we find additional laws and functions, such as feelings, consciousness, insight, the ability to make decisions, and language. How body and soul are connected remains a mystery. All attempts at creating explanatory images, such as that of the body being the dwelling place of the soul in this life, seem inadequate – the human soul will always be a source of great mystery and wonder. The highest level, the spiritual plane, comprises laws and functions over and above those already considered, including faith, intuition, dreaming, prayer, meditation, awareness and consultation.

Considering the world in terms of these five planes of existence can help us refine our image of the functions and faculties typical of humankind. Promoting our own development relies heavily on the functions associated with the highest plane, particularly our insight, language and consciousness, which we must use to help us learn to express our thoughts more precisely, and to evolve a more realistic value system for our actions.

Many issues central to our lives today can be understood at several planes and can even have different meanings within a single plane. 'Love', for instance, can mean many things depending which plane of love is intended. Love on the human plane can refer to the love we have for our friends, our parents or our partner, all of which we would describe differently. On the spiritual level, we could include our love for ourselves; if we are religious, our love of God, or the love we have for the community of humanity of which we are a part. A similar distinction occurs with the term 'freedom'. When we speak of freedom do we mean inner or outer freedom? Are we talking about freedom from something, or the freedom to do something? It depends which plane we are talking about. Or consider 'obedience'. On the animal plane, obedience is central as animals always obey their instincts; they do not have the conscious ability to ignore them. But on the human level, we do have the choice to be obedient or not. As children, obedience is a fairly simple issue – we either obey those who take care of us or not, our disobedience being as much a result of wilfulness as anything more serious. But as we grow up, obedience becomes a far more complex issue, becoming associated with human rights and our insight into the importance of social equality between people. Our decisions whether to obey or not will depend on issues such as whether we desire the outcome obedience will bring, whether we think the request is morally or ethically appropriate, and whether we respect the individual or institution that has issued the demand. Furthermore, on the spiritual plane, which, for the religious, connects humanity with God, obedience is a supreme virtue.

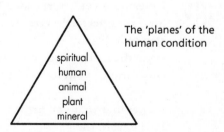

The 'planes' of the human condition

spiritual
human
animal
plant
mineral

In practising personal development, we must take a holistic view, ensuring that we tackle all 'planes' of ourselves, to find a balance between these aspects of our being.

For of the soul the body form doth take;
For soul is form, and doth the body make.

Edmund Spenser

Know thou the soul as riding in a chariot,
The body as the chariot.
Know thou the intellect as the chariot-driver,
And the mind as the reins.

Katha Upanishad

Neglecting or overemphasizing one or more aspects may lead to behaviour that has negative consequences. For instance, functions on the animal plane are the outer senses: sight, hearing, smell, taste and touch, so animals can perceive. But, using their inner senses, such as imagining, thinking, understanding and remembering, humans can *apperceive*, that is, integrate new conscious knowledge into the knowledge that already exists. The appropriate use of these inner senses leads to true knowledge, love, belief and action: the path to spirituality. If we do not use our inner senses appropriately, this will lead us to prejudices such as impulsiveness, emotionality and aggression, attitudes which are undignified and destructive for our personal development.

Tips

Be optimistic.
Determine your purpose in life.
Strive for perfection but take it one step at a time.
Have the courage to be imperfect.
Encourage yourself and encourage others.
Remember that you are unique.
Learn from the past.

2 exploring our spiritual nature

When we read newspapers, magazines or books, or even look through information leaflets produced by business consultants, we come across the terms 'spirit', 'spiritual' and 'spirituality' more and more frequently. In the past, these terms were more or less limited to discussions about religious issues, but they now play an increasingly significant role in the everyday lives of all of us, and have become particularly associated with New Age spirituality. But what does 'spirituality' actually mean? Is the human spirit the same as the soul, or is spirituality exclusively associated with belief in a supreme divine being, God?

Having considered the psychological view of human nature in Chapter 1, we will now turn to this spiritual, or 'inner' view, as it is an important source of knowledge about the individual. As we have discussed, each individual is an entity comprising body, soul and spirit. With technological advances in health, we now know a great deal about our bodies, and can expect to live much longer than would have been the case one hundred years ago. But enthusiasm for scientific developments does not mean that mental and spiritual progress should be undervalued, as seems to be the case at present. While rejoicing at the positive improvements scientific discovery can make to human life, and, we hope, the sustainability of our planet, we should concentrate on the positive transformation of the individual. After all, whatever type of society scientific advances create, it is a society intended for human habitation, and it is human values that will ultimately determine whether this new society is a good place to be. We are already learning to perfect ourselves at the level of the soul or mind, but as far as the spirit is concerned, it would seem that our development is only just getting under way. According to Jean Gebser, we are at the end of the intellectual age in which reason has been dominant and are now at the beginning of a new age in which we are to develop spiritual perfection.

This new age is an overcoming of the rational, fading away, epoch.

Jean Gebser

Many people assume that exploring their spiritual nature will involve examining the spiritual teachings of one of the world's major religious traditions. But from which religious traditions should the teachings come? If we select only one tradition, we will not be taking into account the faiths of many people and may be excluding important teachings from which we could all learn. To assume the positions of each religion in turn would also not be a satisfactory solution. But there is far more to our spiritual selves than the teachings of the well-known religious traditions. I describe the spiritual side of human nature as being made up of the three elements of unity: love, insight and faith. We all imagine we know what love means in this context. We have already discussed on pp. 26–7 that love can mean different things according to its different planes and we shall be examining love in more detail in Chapter 4. But what of insight and faith? These are more complex principles to understand, and we shall be exploring them in this chapter. We need to understand all three elements of unity in order to appreciate that their conscious use is as important for promoting individual development as any practical measures we may choose to take. Only then can we focus on the steps that need to be taken in order to achieve stronger self-belief, the subject of Part Two of this book.

recognizing our capacity for insight

What is insight exactly?

mental penetration

Oxford English Dictionary

the power or act of seeing into a situation or into oneself; the act or fact of apprehending the inner nature of things or of seeing intuitively; clear and immediate thinking

Webster's Dictionary

However you may choose to define it, insight is far more than knowledge. If I know something because I have learned or observed or experienced it, I have acquired this knowledge primarily through the faculty of reason. But insight demands other functions in addition to rational thought. Perhaps a few examples will help.

I know that sweets and chocolate are not good for me. Knowing this, however, does not prevent me from eating them. If, on the other hand, I understand and, more importantly, accept, how much they harm my body, then I will not succumb to the temptation to eat them, or at least will eat fewer sweets. It is often assumed that this merely requires strong will-power, but it has far more to do with insight. Will-power can still let us fool ourselves, whereas we cannot argue with true insight. If I do or do not do something, it is my level of insight that is responsible, whereas concepts such as 'strength' or 'weakness of will' simply provide us with an excuse, albeit one which most people will usually accept.

using our inner senses and our capacity for conscious action

Understanding and tapping into our faculty of insight involves, in particular, acknowledgement of our inner senses. Using our inner senses leads us from knowledge to the insight we need to bring about actions and deeds. The possession of inner senses is a major point of distinction between our animal and human selves. Whenever I perceive something with my outer animal senses – sight, hearing, taste, smell or touch – my first inner human sense, my imagination, will come into play before I can start to think about what I have perceived. The second inner sense is reason. Via rational thought I arrive at the third inner sense, understanding. What I have understood can then be passed into my memory, the fourth inner sense.

The more you understand, the better you can acheive.
Raymond Hull

But who is really aware of these inner senses? Unlike physical sensations we experience, the workings of our inner senses are internal, so it is very easy to be unaware of them. Consciousness could almost be called our fifth inner sense, as it is another exclusively human feature that distinguishes our human from our animal selves. Animals do not have consciousness in the sense that humans do. They unconsciously use the outer senses of sight, hearing, smell, taste and touch, and usually respond to them with an instinctive reaction. Similarly, when a child is born, the animal senses are central – newborn babies concentrate all their efforts on using senses like sight and touch to understand their surroundings. But from an early stage, they will learn to make use of the inner senses, particularly imagination, as they try and impose some order into the sensory messages they are receiving. As they get older, they will become more conscious of their thoughts and actions, and the inner senses of reason, understanding and memory will become increasingly important.

The following examples demonstrate the importance of our inner senses and their inter-relationship with consciousness.

> I am attending a conference and am trying very hard to read the badge of a fellow delegate to determine who she is. By fixing my eyes on the badge, I can recognize and understand simple information about her. But at the same time, I have formed an impression about her as a person and what is important to her. How can I have got so much information from a small badge?

Even though it is the badge that is the object of my attention, and although I am not particularly interested, I also take in a lot of peripheral information about the other delegate. I can see the clothes she has on; furthermore, I see the whole person and part of her surroundings. The further away the surrounding things are from the point on which I am concentrating, the less clear they are to me, and the less conscious I am of them. But that does not mean I have not absorbed them, and have used my imagination to build up a picture based on these visual stimuli. I feel I know a lot about my colleague, but mostly not at a sufficiently conscious level to be able to register my knowledge.

Man knows more than he understands.

Alfred Adler

Here is another example. Think about what this can tell us about the workings of our inner senses.

> A child asks me where clouds come from. I fix my memory on what I have learned about that subject, i.e. that when the humidity of the air reaches a certain point, the water droplets become visible. I also know the names of the different types of clouds, but it is only when a further question from the child about the names of the clouds arises and I see the need to fix on that area of my memory that I can recall the names.

This demonstrates the selective power of memory. There are various types of knowledge or memory – conscious, semiconscious, subconscious, etc. There is far more information available in our minds than we need access to on an everyday basis. As we read in Chapter 1, there are many things in life that we do not always need to be conscious of or that, for reasons of economy, we forget after having once been conscious of them. If we want to walk, for instance, we do not need to consider whether to start with the left or right leg. If we had to be conscious of every such little detail we would never get round to doing anything! However, as this example demonstrates, when we do have a need for infrequently accessed parts of our memory, we can consciously call upon them. We have this facility with all our inner senses – we can consciously summon them to the fore for conscious, active use. This is what we need to do if we are to develop our capacity for insight and understanding with the goal of improving our self-belief, as we shall see later.

Let us consider another example.

> I am introduced to a woman at a party. We chat for a while, and she seems perfectly friendly, but I know straight away that I do not like her. But for all of me, I can't think

why. She smiles and laughs a lot, and has not said anything offensive. So why don't I like her?

I am sure we can all empathize with this response – there
can often be 'something about someone' that makes us
particularly like them or not, for reasons we cannot understand, let alone put into words. Perhaps in this case, it is a
mixture of my memory and imagination acting together
that produces my uncomfortable feeling. Perhaps the person bears a physical or behavioural resemblance to someone I knew in my childhood and whom I did not like. I have
a similar problem when I visit my aunt. I only know that I
never feel like visiting her, but I do not consciously realize
that my reluctance is due to her habit of constantly
putting me down. This makes me feel awkward and
unsure of myself in her presence.

This sort of uncertainty happens with a lot of our problems. It is like when we are gardening, we see the leaves
of weeds and remove them without worrying too much
about the fact that the weed has broken off before the
roots came up. We know our weeding efforts are pointless
unless we pull out the roots, but we accept the short-term
option because everything looks superficially 'tidy'.

the importance of faith

Having explored what is meant by insight, we will now
examine the third element of unity, faith. The concept of
belief, or faith, is used in many different ways. When
someone says, 'I believe we're in for a hot summer', they
mean that they are of the opinion that the coming summer will be hot. This is the most common meaning of the
verb 'to believe' and indicates that the person expressing
their view does not or cannot know something for certain,
but has a strong opinion.

When I discuss faith, however, I am referring to it as a typically human faculty on the spiritual plane, like thinking and feeling. Most people are only aware of this kind of faith in a religious context. Indeed it was the kind of faith that Jesus Christ was referring to when he told someone he had healed that

'Thy faith hath made thee whole.'

Holy Bible, Luke 17:19

This demonstrates how the power of faith has always been recognized in religion, but it is also well known in the medical profession, where tests using placebos (inactive substances made to look and taste like genuine medication) demonstrate that the efficacy of a drug depends very heavily on whether or not the patient taking it has faith in its power to heal.

Nevertheless, most of us are not aware that the power of faith, or what we call in Individual Psychology *the power of expectation* or *power of anticipation*, is probably the greatest power we can have. We all make use of this power from morning to night – indeed most of what we do is connected with our faculty of faith – but we are rarely aware of doing so. I get up in the morning because I believe that it is better for me than lying in bed doing nothing. The same belief leads me to wash myself, comb my hair, take exercise and put on clean clothes. I only have a small breakfast because I believe my stomach appreciates not having to do a lot of digestion in the morning. My business partner prefers to eat a full breakfast because he believes this is better for him. This would not do for me because my beliefs differ from his in this matter. We both believe that what we do is best for us and does not harm anyone else, with no feelings of inferiority or superiority involved. After breakfast, I sit down at my desk to work on a book that I believe may help some people cope better with their problems and have a happier life. After that I go into my consulting room to meet patients who, I believe, are prepared to let me help them. As this demonstrates, faith is more than just hope. It is the only way of achieving certainty.

He that hath faith hath wisdom; he that hath wisdom hath peace. He that hath no wisdom and no faith, whose soul is one of doubt, is destroyed.

Mahabharata

Because we constantly use our power of faith, but usually not consciously, it sometimes occurs that we use the faculty when it is not appropriate, or when it supports us in our egocentric behaviour and/or in a way that is harmful to communal life.

overcoming negative faith

Because our faculty of faith is usually used unconsciously, we are often aware of it only in a negative form. Just as positive faith can help us achieve the desirable things we aspire to, lack of faith can very often bring about the very things of which we are afraid – it is as if by not believing in a particular positive outcome, we are willing it not to happen. For example, if we believe we will not manage something, we probably will not; if we believe others are going to be hostile towards us, they probably will be.

Geoff is 53, married to a wife he loves dearly, and has two teenage children. But he is making his own and his family's lives difficult through his nervousness, sleeping difficulties and alcohol problems. Guilt is racking his conscience because decades ago, early on in his marriage, he once slept with another woman. His wife knows and has long since forgiven him, but this does not prevent him falling into ever deeper states of depression.

If Geoff had more faith in himself, he could say to himself that he cannot undo his past deed but that he can make sure nothing similar ever happens again. Indeed, he has not made the same mistake since. But he has too little faith in himself, his wife, the present and the future, with the result that his capacity for love and insight have also been unable to develop.

Trish is a very attractive married woman in her mid-forties, who has recently developed a powerful fear of growing old. This fear has been intensified by her discovery of grey hairs on her head. She tries to hide these and is thinking of having her hair dyed. She is extremely depressed and considers her life to be practically meaningless. Up to now, her main aim in life has been to gain admiration from men and to feel superior to other women. She is always concerned with herself, her body and her appearance and has not developed her intellectual or spiritual capacities. Trish's husband, Chris, who has had a successful professional career, has made it possible for her to enjoy life and take advantage of all the pleasures his success has afforded. They do not have any children, nor any close friends, but have a large circle of acquaintances.

We discussed on p. 22 how discouragement can lead to egocentricity, and this is what has happened to Geoff and Trish. Both of them need to move from egocentricity to self-belief, and encourage each other on the journey. But how can they, or any of us, learn to believe? This too takes an initial step of faith – I will never learn if I 'know' from the start that I cannot change. But how much or how little one believes is a conscious decision that each individual can make. Just as a salesperson first has to buy merchandise in advance, not knowing whether he or she will succeed in selling it at a profit, I have to invest faith irrespective of whether or not the outcome of my investment pays off in the way I would wish. Things cannot always go right and it is in the nature of things that human beings are not machines, but alive, and their lives involve ups and downs.

the path of spiritualization

As we have established, we look to the spiritual sides of our nature to give us the vital insight to inspire the process that can turn aspiration and intention into actions and deeds. In order to undertake this search for insight successfully, we have to follow what can be called 'the path of spiritualization'. This is the path from egocentricity to self-belief, from self-centredness to open-hearted spiritual awareness. Where the self-centred person searches in vain to find the meaning *in* life, the spiritual person who has travelled the path of spiritualization has recognized that it is up to him or her to give meaning *to* life. Rather than misusing the past in order to wage conflict in the present, the spiritual person uses the past to shape a positive present and has faith in the future.

Just as the path to perfection should be taken in small steps, the path to spiritualization should be tackled in achievable stages – if you are not used to exploring your spiritual self, you cannot expect to reach your destination in one leap! Although we are concentrating on our spiritual being, it is important to take care of one's body, to ensure it functions well and is well prepared for the journey. A good diet is essential, involving as many natural, fresh products as possible. Fluid intake must be frequent and regular, accompanied by plenty of fresh air and exercise.

As well as physical readiness, spiritualization requires our other capacities. We need access to our capacities for love and insight and therefore need both our brain and our heart. Spiritual, religious and psychological literature can also be of assistance. But the starting point on the path of spiritualization must be to invest our faculty of faith in order to increase our ability to believe. Investing faith means consciously deciding to use this faculty. The main point is that we make the conscious decision to believe that we can learn to determine our own selves, our lives and our destinies.

using our decision-making powers

Like our inner senses and our consciousness, the ability to make decisions is a typically human faculty and a power of inestimable significance. Whatever we think, feel, believe, hope, wish for, do or do not do depends on a decision we have made, though most of us make very few such decisions consciously. No one but myself can produce my thoughts and feelings. However, I can decide consciously to use the presence, the words or behaviour of other people as a trigger for their production. If we can recognize this unique decision-making power and apply it consciously, we can enjoy boundless inner freedom, in stark contrast to our external, or physical, freedom which must be limited to some extent if we are to live unselfishly together in peace and equality.

Conscious decision-making is the key to a life in which we achieve our aims and satisfy our hopes, but, like so many other things in life, decision-making becomes easier with practice. Newborn babies, like animals, react impulsively to environmental stimuli, and are not immediately able to use their faculty of conscious decision-making. But because of its vital importance, parents should encourage their children to make small decisions as early as possible. Practice in the early years of life will prepare children for making more important decisions later on, and will give them a strengthened sense of self-belief to carry forward into adulthood.

taking responsibility

The key to utilizing your conscious decision-making powers to achieve positive change is to accept responsibility for your actions, to take on board that it is *your* task to be an instrument of change in your life. So many people fail in making conscious decisions because they have always made most of their decisions unconsciously and they cannot or will not make the necessary lateral jump to initiate decisions. Plus it is so easy, either blatantly or, again, unconsciously, to hold other people or circumstances responsible for our decisions, either denying or often plainly avoiding responsibility. It is easy to transfer the responsibility onto others. We rely on institutions – schools, social services, government – to be responsible for our lives, and therefore neglect our own responsibilities. It is true that these institutions have a role to play – after all, it is the collective power of individuals, for the most part, that has established them – but we must also accept our personal responsibility for both our own development and that of the world. There is a limit to what anyone can do in the face of world crises – individuals and institutions are helpless in the face of current world problems, and sometimes it seems like the cycles of war and famine will never cease – but equally, if no one did anything, situations would be even worse.

Denial of responsibility may have its roots in childhood. Children whose parents did everything, and who therefore had few opportunities to develop their own capabilities, powers and self-responsibility, may be particularly prone to refusing to accept responsibility for their adult lives. They may prefer to let their parents retain responsibility, or they may 'replace' their parents with another person whom they can hold responsible for the progress of their life, perhaps a partner or another older adult. Or they may just blame circumstances for everything, saying that the world is against them and that what is happening to them 'isn't anything to do with me'.

But when people begin to appreciate the potential of their decision-making faculty and can appreciate the benefits that exercising it can bring, most seize responsibility for their own behaviour. If we take full responsibility for our actions, we can make more decisions at a conscious level, and achieve positive change in our lives. Many people attribute their lack of self-worth to circumstances or the behaviour of others, but if you are to take positive steps to improve your self-belief, you have to believe that it is within your remit to actualize that change. Simply by buying this book you are halfway there, but consciously telling yourself, out loud if you like, that improving your self-esteem is *your* job, no one else's, will help you reach your goal.

Responsibility for humanity – both as a collection of unique individuals and as a collective whole – is shared. Each one of us is responsible for our own personal growth, for nurturing our own development, but we are all also responsible for encouraging the development of those around us, and ultimately for humanity as a whole.

controlling our emotions

What do we mean when we talk about emotions? Are emotions the same as feelings, or is there some distinction, and if so, what is it? Both words refer to strong, inner, responses. For the purposes of this book, when I refer to 'emotions', I mean 'negative feelings', feelings that are irrational, not constructive, and which may cause disturbances to life in human society. I refer to reactions like jealousy, resentment, and so forth. 'Feelings', on the other hand, refer to responses that have a positive outcome, such as love.

In our present-day society, we are encouraged to give free rein to our emotions. We are told that we have to be 'in touch' with our emotions to understand our true psychological state – our motivations and ambitions. There is no doubt that suppressing one's emotions is not a good idea – we can all think of children we know, who, motivated by the unconscious goal of achieving a sense of belonging, learn early to suppress their emotions or desires to satisfy the expectations of those around them. At the same time, giving free rein to our emotions can be just as detrimental to family and community life. If I let my emotional response control my speech and actions, I can easily violate the dignity of others and cause unnecessary upset or offence, which, particularly in a close-knit family situation, can cause unwanted tension and animosity for a prolonged period.

It is perfectly possible to be 'in touch' with one's emotions without being their slave.

Emotions should be servants, not masters – or at least not tyrants.

Robert Hugh Benson

At the same time as being aware of the emotional response we are experiencing, we can use our conscious decision-making faculty to decide to react in a less emotional way and choose a more constructive mode of behaviour. The less we let our emotions take the lead, the less we will find ourselves needing to look for excuses to justify ourselves. Again, the enormous power and potential of a more conscious approach to decision-making can change our lives for the better, allowing us to exercise control over our emotions without suppressing them. In this way we can enjoy greater freedom of feeling, thought and action, without suffering the frustration and anguish either of suppressed emotion or of pain at the negative consequences of an emotionally driven outburst.

the emotions and our inner senses

If I do not use my inner senses consciously, it is very likely that I will respond emotionally, with negative consequences. The following case demonstrates what I mean.

> I hear my small daughter using a swear-word. This is not the first time this has happened and my immediate response is to shout at her with displeasure. Her reaction is to stare me in the face and say the offending word repeatedly before running off crying.

What has happened here is that I have reacted impulsively and emotionally with annoyance and displeasure. The consequences are negative – my daughter is crying and has therefore not learned from the experience, so is likely to swear in the future. Impulsive reactions like these turn me into my daughter's plaything because I let my behaviour be determined by her words rather than my own goals, and thus have abandoned my role as educator. In this situation, my daughter has become more powerful than me. What I should have done, but was too lazy to do, was to call on my inner sense of imagination. I should have passed on what I had heard, via my imagination, to my faculty of reason in order to understand why my daughter had uttered the undesirable words. What was she trying to achieve? I would then have realized that what she said was of subordinate significance and that what she really wanted was my affection or attention. At that moment she had decided that swearing was the best way of achieving this. By calling on my inner senses, I could have turned this situation into a positive one in which I would have learned more about my child and what motivates her. I could also have tried to educate her about what is acceptable and unacceptable speech. Instead, the child's offending behaviour has been immediately repeated; I just have tears and a very unresponsive daughter with whom I shall have trouble communicating for at least the next hour.

thinking for ourselves

Just as it is all too easy to give others responsibility for your life and deny your own role in determining an outcome, it is also the easy route to allow your thoughts to be prescribed to you by others. Again, if you do not use your decision-making faculty when it comes to thoughts, all you are doing is reacting to the words or behaviour of other people. By doing so, you are continuing in a direction set by someone else. We can all imagine the following scenario.

There is an election next month. Every evening on the television, I see and hear the spokespersons of the various political parties involved speaking about issues and policies, trying to convince us all that they are right and the other parties wrong. After listening to one, very professionally put-together broadcast, I am convinced that the party in question are right – they are saying things that largely seem to agree with my views and I agree with what they want to achieve. But the next night I hear another broadcast. What this party says seems right too – they are following a common-sense line, and I am sure they are right, and I decide they will receive my vote the following week.

In this situation, I have just let myself 'go with the flow'. Of course both accounts sound credible – the press officers of these political parties are professionals, and it is their job to make the messages their broadcasts communicate convincing. Instead of letting the most recent impression persist, allowing someone else to construct our thoughts for us, we should decide to consider the arguments of both sides ourselves, to use our rational inner sense. We may come to the conclusion that neither of them has the right answer.

Unless we start to think for ourselves, Einstein's prediction that 'If humanity is not prepared to rethink its views, to find a different, new way of thinking, it is doomed to perish' will come true. We are frequently unwilling to think differently, to abandon our customary decision-making systems, because we have too little faith in ourselves and our ability to think. We are afraid to take on board anything new, deeming it better to cling to our old ways of thinking, since what we know well gives us a feeling of security. New ideas may threaten us, but we should seize them as new opportunities, as possible new tools to help us along our path of personal development. New tools are the gateway to a new life. Think of the new 'tools' of the past century that have radically altered our lives – the telephone, the car, the personal computer – and what it would have been like if we had shied away from these technological departures and not seized the opportunities they offered. You must seize the new and use it to forge a brighter future.

prejudice

It is the absence of independent thought, of an individual forming their own opinions, that can lead to prejudice.

Prejudice is born of impersonal second-hand thinking which arises because we pass on what we have perceived to our imagination but no further. Again, we are too idle to subject it to personal consideration, to our own rational thought.

[Prejudice –]an opinion without judgement.

Voltaire

I simply follow what I have perceived, thus making myself dependent on the opinions of others and neglecting to use my faculty of insight. I remain at the stage of simple, empty knowledge; in other words, at the level of ideas and vain imaginings. In so doing I am hindering my personal development. Thinking for yourself, using your inner senses to go beyond pure knowledge to positive insight, will help you refine your thought processes and lead you to more precise conclusions and actions from your thoughts and experiences.

having the right attitude

The success of much of what we have covered in this chapter depends on the attitude of the individual, particularly towards his or her own capacities and what the future may hold. You have to have the right attitude to dig down and use your inner senses rather than let your emotions have sway, to form your own thoughts and opinions rather than just assimilate those of others, to take responsibility for the course of your life rather than rely on others. The important point is that, using your reason, you can consciously change your attitude for the purposes you seek to achieve. Just as you can consciously decide to use your decision-making powers or to react less emotionally to circumstances, so you can exercise more control throughout your life.

Tips

Acknowledge and use your inner senses.
Be aware of your power of faith.
Accept responsibility for your actions.
Learn to control your emotions whilst acknowledging your feelings.
Let go of habitual thinking.

part two

The Steps to Take

Having established the principles upon which enhanced self-belief is based – the tools that you will use on your journey to self-confidence – the rest of this book explores the steps you can take to improve your self-belief – the practical and spiritual skills you can apply to your life to fulfil your true potential.

3 learning to make fine distinctions

In today's world, we are surrounded by a haze of complex and varied messages and signals. They come from many different sources – the obvious ones come from the media, advertising and the world of business and commerce, but even interpersonal relationships are far more complex than they were fifty years ago, and we have to get used to receiving complicated messages from friends, family and even our partner. These complex signals demand of each of us a more refined ability to make distinctions, greater precision in our reasoning and self-expression, and more clarity in our attitudes and in our recognition of the planes of existence (see pp. 25–8). Without these developments our perception can become 'muddy', and we can make ourselves believe things that are not true, both about ourselves and others, and can become guilty of giving out mixed messages ourselves. This can lead to conflict and resentment between the closest people, and self-belief is diminished rather than strengthened.

In this chapter, we will look at the most common false distinctions, and examine how we can ensure that we exercise our powers of recognition appropriately to maintain sense and balance both within ourselves and in our relationships with others. The order of presentation of the different distinctions is of no significance.

mistakes versus mistaken attitudes

There is an important difference between mistakes and mistaken attitudes. To err is to be human – everyone makes mistakes, and should not set too much store by them. More often than not we can make up for our mistakes in some way. If people try never to make a mistake, they will end up in a state of discouragement, because they are trying to go beyond their human limitations, a path which is doomed to fail.

> *The man who makes no mistakes does not usually make anything.*
>
> Edward John Phelps

On the other hand, if people are not prepared to learn from their mistakes and to turn major faults into minor ones; in other words, if they have a mistaken attitude, they will keep making the same mistakes over and over again. It is therefore important not only to work on minimizing our mistakes, but also on abandoning our mistaken attitudes. Clinging to mistaken attitudes can hinder not only our own personal development, but as we often project our mistaken opinions and priorities onto others, we can also disrupt the personal development of those we care about. A mistaken attitude is also almost always a means of pursuing – usually unconsciously, of course – one of the five short-term goals, which we discussed on pp.15–16.

caution versus fear

To approach something with caution is a sign of intelligence, even wisdom, and is therefore nearly always right.

If, on the other hand, I tackle a task, or confront a situation, out of fear, or with fear in my heart, then I am questioning the likely success of the enterprise right from the start. Unfortunately, many people confuse caution with fear, not realizing that the latter is a negative approach. Caution and apprehension can stimulate us to act at our best, whereas fear, born of uncertainty or self-doubt, is likely to bring about the very outcome we are afraid of.

Quidquid agas, prudenter agas, et respice finem.
Whatever you do do cautiously, and look to the end.

Anon

A well-known example involves the relationship between humans and domestic animals. The way that pets can sense fear is well documented – a dog in the presence of a child who is afraid of it will be provoked and is likely to act aggressively, just as the child fears. The child will then feel that it is right to be afraid. However, if pets are approached with a combination of assertiveness and caution, they will believe themselves in the presence of a superior rather than inferior 'animal' and are unlikely to be aggressive.

kindness versus firmness

Many people are very good at being kind, but not at being firm; others are good at being firm, but are not kind; most people can be both kind and firm, but not at the same time. Knowing when to be kind and when to be firm is an important life skill. Being kind, both to oneself and to others, is a virtue and we should not seek to change our kindly attitude. However, there are times when we must be firm. These occur both in our relationships with others, particularly our children, and in relation to ourselves, for example in doing what we think is right, particularly when faced with a difficult situation where the temptation to go for the easy path is very strong.

> Simon has an aggressive boss, who only ever gives instructions by shouting and making Simon feel incompetent and undervalued. One day, he yells out to Simon to carry out a certain task on a project they have been working on. Simon has done more work on the project than his boss, and he really feels that the task his boss is referring to would be better done in a different way. He suggests this to his boss, saying he will look into it and get back to him, and calmly leaves his boss's office. Having examined the relevant information, he decides his own opinion was right, and informs his boss of his proposed alternative course of action, clearly stating his reasons. His boss is aggressive in response, but cannot argue with Simon's presentation of his case and approves his plan.

It would have been easiest for Simon just to carry out his boss's instructions as they were given, however inappropriate he may have considered them, but Simon would have felt resentful towards his boss and had little respect for himself. Simon did not directly contradict his boss's instructions from the outset because this would have led to a quarrel; rather, he remained friendly and respectful, saying, 'You may well be right; I will look into this and get back to you', giving his boss appropriate credit. After he had considered his boss's instructions, he might have come to the conclusion that the instructions were justified, in which case he would have told his boss that he was right and would have carried the instructions through. Throughout the episode, Simon's behaviour was both kind and firm, and it succeeded in getting him (and ultimately his boss) what he wanted, without causing any real harm to his boss's or his own feelings. His firmness also succeeded in neutralizing any feelings of resentment that he might have felt at his boss's unreasonable behaviour as well as making Simon feel better about himself. A certain amount of self-belief is a prerequisite for being able to use kindness and firmness as appropriately as Simon did. However, as Simon's experience also demonstrates, the effective use of kindness and firmness, even in a small degree, in our everyday lives, can help our sense of self-belief and self-worth to develop.

understanding and helping versus arguing and surrendering

If I argue with someone, I violate his or her dignity; if I surrender, I insult my own. Neither of these options can be right. If I believe in the social equality of all people, then I have a duty to respect my own worth and that of others equally. This principle of mutual respect leads to a third option: understanding and helping. Understanding is a prerequisite to helping – before I can help, I must understand what the problem is. The key to understanding is thinking about which short-term goal a person is pursuing, as we discussed on pp. 15–16.

Having understood is not yet a guarantee that I will know what to do in a given situation. But there is one thing I can always do, and that is to decide to engage an attitude of wishing to help. External circumstances may prevent me from actually helping, because they or other people are stronger than me, but nothing and no one can prevent me from wanting to help. Maintaining an attitude of wanting to help is an important tool in nurturing self-belief. Whether or not I actually succeed in helping, I should feel good about myself for trying to take the right path, and the other person will respect my efforts.

taking things with composure versus giving in

It is definitely true that we should not surrender in a way that threatens our sense of self-worth, but at the same time it is important to accept when we are wrong. We should all know when to stop, when to accept that we are tilting at windmills and that the time has come to back down with composure. Far from showing weakness, knowing when to step back and accept the reality of a situation is one of the strongest signs of self-belief, a real sign of insight and intelligence.

agreement versus contradiction

If someone expresses a fallacious opinion, it is very difficult not either to contradict directly and cause unnecessary conflict, or to agree for a quiet life, inwardly seething that you have not managed to get across your point of view. I am sure most of us will recognize the following scenario, or have experienced a similar one.

> Alison is at a party, and is discussing with a group of people the latest policy announced by the government. It happens to be an issue about which Alison feels particularly strongly and she believes that, for once, the government has chosen an appropriate course of action. Much to Alison's annoyance, a man in the group, who she finds particularly arrogant and believes plainly knows nothing about the subject, has taken over the conversation and is expressing opinions which she feels are misguided. How should she react?

There is no point in Alison contradicting the man. He, like anyone else, would not accept correction from someone who appeared to believe she knew better; he would feel personally threatened and also irritated by his perception of her arrogance. But equally, Alison should not stay silent as that would be a denial of the strength of her views and detrimental to her self-belief. The correct attitude is for Alison first to listen with interest to what the man says and then agree in some form – we have all heard people use expressions like 'I see what you mean, but . . .' – even if what the other person is saying may at first appear to be nonsense. In a situation like this, Alison must respect the fact that, from the other person's point of view, he is right, while at the same time making it clear that she believes he does not see the whole picture. Her partial agreement is not dishonest, nor does it mean that she is turning back on her own views; it just means that she is showing due respect to an equal human being's point of view. To broaden the picture, she could ask whether the opinion he is expressing would also be appropriate in a related situation. In this way the man will realize that Alison is not trying to assert her superiority, but rather is striving to establish equality. He should listen to her, think about the situation she has described, and can then reach his own conclusion. He may decide that his original opinion was not quite correct but needed to be complemented, or he may hold on to his view. Either way, both he and Alison have retained their belief in themselves, allowing each other to retain their feelings of self-worth whilst avoiding the need to demonstrate superiority.

power versus force

Whether the use of force is ever appropriate is a hot ethical issue, with many people believing force can only be right when it springs from a pure motive – for the good of others, for example. Others do not believe it can ever be justly employed. It is important, however, to distinguish between force, which is so often an instrument of oppression, and power, which, used appropriately, and in the hands of the right people, can be an instrument for good, and protects the world from corruption.

Power at its best is love implementing the demands of justice.
Martin Luther King

Power should be used appropriately in our personal relationships too. Rather than force our colleagues, friends, or partners to do something out of a sense of fear or inferiority, we should use the power that is born of the strength of the relationship to achieve the desired goal in a spirit of mutual respect.

requesting versus demanding

In a partnership of any kind, it is always wrong to demand something from the other person; rather, if I need something from someone else I should ask for it politely. If I request rather than demand, I am affirming my self-belief rather than making it obvious that I need to assert some sort of superior status in order to get what I want. In addition, whether you are in a loving relationship, or are a manager in a business environment, you are far more likely to receive what you are hoping for if you ask for it rather than demand it. Your partner or colleagues will respond out of love and/or respect for you, whereas a demand will only elicit negative feelings of subordination and hostility.

cooperation versus dictation

This is a similar distinction to the one above, but this one is particularly relevant in relationships between individuals that, it may be argued, may not be on an even footing, such as parents and children, teachers and students or managers and employees. In the past, the 'superior' party in these kinds of relationships would demand cooperation from the 'inferior' party; even today many think that dictating action is more effective than winning cooperation from others, arguing that this method inculcates a sense of respect. But in today's society, this approach is less and less successful as people, whether children or adults, expect to be, and respond more cooperatively to being, treated as equals.

Any attempt to convince others to behave in a certain way therefore, whether it be trying to persuade your children to do their homework, students to pay attention, or an employee to carry out a particular task, is more likely to be effective if the person(s) in question are on your team rather than feeling in opposition to you. In other words, if they feel that you and they are cooperating, working towards the same goal, rather than acting in opposition. It is therefore worthwhile always ensuring that relationships of all kinds are conducted in a spirit of unity and cooperation, as this will help all parties progress to agreed goals and live and work together in a positive way.

being dependent on others versus being determined by them

It is one of the positive elements of modern society that individuals can make their own decisions about themselves and their lives, irrespective of the dependence relationships in which they find themselves. I am dependent on my family but I need not be determined by it. Everyone goes through a number of dependence relationships in their lives, the most obvious being the child–parent relationship, where the child depends on the parent for both its physical and spiritual well-being. Later in life we may find ourselves dependent on a partner for our general happiness and well-being, and on our employers for our financial security. We are even dependent on the shops in which we buy what we need to feed and clothe ourselves. However, although we may be dependent on these relationships, we are not determined by them; the dependence may be strong but this does not mean that the other person or people in the relationship have the right to make our decisions for us. Fortunately the days are gone when employers could determine the personal aspects of the lives of their employees.

How we are determined comes from within – only we have the right to determine what makes us who we are, how we should live our lives, and what we should be aiming for. As we discussed in Chapter 2, accepting and seizing responsibility for how we live our lives, and not letting other people make these decisions for us, is a crucial aspect of developing our self-belief.

experience versus facts

In certain fields of life, such as law or medicine, for example, facts are of central importance. Far more significant in the life of an individual, however, is the way in which he or she experiences a particular situation; in other words, his or her interpretation of what some would describe as 'facts'. The same situation may be experienced very differently by the people involved, and all parties must be aware of this and be sensitive to how another's interpretation of a situation may differ from their own.

In most relationships, failure to make the distinction between fact and experience is a common cause of argument and conflict. Most of us will have experienced situations where we have disagreed with a colleague or partner over what one or other of us has previously said, both of us sticking adamantly to our story. Part of sustaining a successful relationship is acknowledging that in situations such as these there is rarely such a thing as a fact; it is because the views of both parties are so strong that facts appear to be involved. Rather than dismiss the other person's point of view, we should ensure that we helpfully apply the policy of agreeing rather than contradicting to ensure that conflict does not develop, or, if it does, to help dispel it in a spirit of love and cooperation.

empathy versus pity

If I pity someone, it can often give them the feeling that they are inferior to me – that I feel sorry for the predicament in which they find themselves, but am at the same time either relieved that it has not happened to me, or even a little unsympathetic because I would not have let it happen to me in the first place. If, on the other hand, I express empathy, this means that not only do I understand the other person's feelings, but I also engage my own feelings in what they are experiencing and attempt to share and participate at an equal level in their difficulty. This tightens the bonds between us and is more likely to encourage the other person to find a way out of the difficulty rather than to feel rejected and negative. Empathy can therefore reinforce the self-belief of both people involved – both the person that expresses empathy, and the person who receives it.

To [empathize with] the unhappy is not contrary to self-ish desire; on the other hand, we are glad of the occasion to thus testify friendship and attract to ourselves the reputation of tenderness, without giving anything.

Pascal

guidance versus domination

Most of us will at some point find ourselves in situations where we feel in need of the guidance of others, or others seek guidance from us. In both these situations it is important to distinguish between guidance and domination. When we seek guidance, that is all we are seeking – we are capable of making the necessary decisions ourselves, but maybe just need a friend to 'bounce' ideas off, to share our thought-processes with, to help us clarify our real feelings. We are not looking for someone to take our problems out of our hands and dominate what we do, thereby assuming a superior position and depriving us of the important responsibility we have for dictating what happens to us. Similarly, if we are asked for guidance, it is even more important to take care not to dominate, which may be very tempting if the person seems weak and incapable of dealing with their problems. If we give in to the temptation to dominate, we will be depriving the individual of whatever little bit of self-belief they may have left. In being asked to guide, it is our responsibility to treat our troubled friend as an equal, enhancing his or her self-belief rather than further damaging it.

deed versus doer

Since perfection is an unattainable goal (see pp. 20–1), we cannot be sure that our actions will always be flawless; indeed, we can be pretty sure that this will not be the case. However, when people do make mistakes, they should not be devalued; they are still human beings with a right to the respect and recognition of others. The worst imaginable deeds are perpetrated by human beings, and regardless of what someone does, however inhuman I may consider their actions, that person is and will always remain a fellow human being of equal status to myself, for whom I share a certain responsibility. Rejection of the deed does not mean rejection of the doer. He or she needs the help of others, whether it is accepted or not; hatred of the doer will achieve nothing, and at worst will encourage further destructive deeds to be committed.

Distinguishing between deed and doer is important in all aspects of society. At a national and international level, it is one of the most powerful distinctions we need to make if we are concerned to improve the life of the society we live in; it guides us towards a fair justice system, for example. It is also important in our everyday relationships. There are very few of us who do not feel we have been let down at some stage by the actions of someone very close to us. When it happens, it is all too easy to dismiss the person along with the deed, as we try to convince ourselves that they did not value the relationship in the way we thought, and that we had always misunderstood them. But inside we know this is not usually the case and we should endeavour to distance ourselves from the single deed that has offended us and re-establish and nurture what to date has been a good relationship. John, in the example below, is faced with this sort of challenge:

Sarah is due to go on a foreign holiday with some friends, which involves a two-and-a-half hour flight. Her partner, John, is more than happy for her to go, but has always been nervous about planes, and will be relieved when he knows Sarah has arrived safely. As always they agree that she will phone when she gets to the hotel, and work out roughly what sort of time that will be. Sarah goes off to the airport, very excited about her holiday.

The following day, as the earliest time Sarah might phone approaches, John is not too worried as he knows flight delays happen all too often. But as the hours go by, and each time the phone goes it is not Sarah, he begins to get more and more concerned. After twelve hours, he is extremely worried and phones Sarah's parents, but they have not heard from her either. He decides to phone the tour operator to see if the plane has arrived safely. Much to his relief, it has, but he is still wondering why Sarah has not phoned him. When she finally phones, she is very apologetic, and says, 'Oh, you know how it is – once we got to the hotel, we just wanted to get unpacked and look around – I completely forgot to phone; I am sorry.'

In this situation, John is obviously hurt at his partner's blatant lack of consideration. There is no denying that she is at fault, but selfishness is not a common trait in Sarah, and John is able to accept that her behaviour was brought on by her excitement at the holiday and is in no way a reflection of her overall character or of her feelings for him. He knows she will be feeling guilty enough as it is without him making an issue of things. He agrees with her that she was wrong, but accepts her apology and is just relieved that she is safe.

The ability not to take issue in a situation such as this reinforces our self-belief and is also a source of support for the other person involved. As I have said previously in this book, the more we believe in ourselves, the more we can believe in others, and the more we can encourage one another.

spontaneity versus impulsiveness

This is one of the more difficult distinctions to make as spontaneity and impulsiveness are actually quite similar, though there are some crucial differences. One way of trying to explain the distinction is to describe spontaneity as 'positive impulsiveness' and impulsiveness as 'negative spontaneity'. Both involve an absence of premeditation, but impulsiveness tends to involve more of a renunciation of control. An impulsive response can be a totally unconsidered reaction to a whim or sudden event, and can be completely out of character with the individual's usual patterns of behaviour. The negative aspect of impulsiveness is also demonstrated by the fact that it tends to be emotionally driven and, as we discussed on p. 43, emotionally-driven speech and behaviour can cause disturbances in human relationships. On the other hand, spontaneous behaviour comes from the inside and, unlike impulsiveness, relies on the use of the inner senses. As such, it is unlikely to be out of character with the person's usual character, and will conform to his or her beliefs of what is right, through insight, love and faith.

The positive nature of spontaneity versus the negative nature of impulsiveness is clearer to understand if you consider a parent's possible reactions to a child's behaviour. An impulsive reaction by a mother, for example, might lead her to discipline her child harshly for a mild misdemeanour. A spontaneous reaction, on other hand, might involve her snatching her child out of danger or suggesting an impromptu trip to the seaside, which will give pleasure to the whole family.

talking *to* versus *at* each other

This difference may seem attributable to just a couple of letters, but the difference between talking *to* and talking *at* is immense. Talking *to*, or *with*, another person involves equal and mutual respect and kindness – the establishment of a 'we' from an equal 'you' and 'I' – whereas talking *at* another is a device used by people who seek to establish their superiority. We all know what being talked at is like – that in itself should be enough to stop us doing it!

Everyone can learn how to talk to, rather than at, others, provided they establish an equal relationship. This can be achieved by taking account of the following. First, you should ensure that both people want the conversation to take place, and that neither party is agreeing against their will to a demand made by the other. Second, it is important that the place where the conversation is taking place does not put either party at a disadvantage. This is particularly important if the conversation is to be on a subject about which the parties do not agree. It is also preferable if a location can be chosen where the individuals will not be disturbed for a reasonable length of time. This will help to fulfil the third condition – that there is a positive atmosphere. Also important is an agreement that the conversation will be broken off if one of the parties becomes angry. The fourth condition is the hardest to fulfil, particularly if the conversation is to be about a difficult subject – one should not try to initiate a conversation with a friend or colleague that confronts a problem he or she has, as this will immediately introduce an inferior–superior dimension to the relationship. The other person will feel accused, put down and/or criticized, and will no longer be interested in the conversation, but only in justifying or defending himself or herself. To ensure an equal, 'talking to' rather than 'talking at' conversation, it is wise only to talk about a problem of one's own. In this way, we are asking the other person for cooperation and assistance, while maintaining an equal relationship.

how I say something versus what I say

The famous English actor David Garrick once held a wager with his friends that he would be able to move his audience to tears merely by reciting the alphabet. He then proceeded to do exactly that, with no one who heard him able to hold back their tears. Garrick won his bet.

This is an extreme example, but it does demonstrate that how one says something is as important, sometimes more so, than what one says. While the words we speak convey our basic message, it is the fine nuances in our tone of voice, our facial expression and our gestures that communicate how we feel about both what we are saying and our relationship with the other person.

It is particularly important to be aware of the importance of how we say something in situations of possible conflict. If our partner regularly does something that annoys us, how much better it would be to say, 'My darling, you know it troubles me when you do that. I know it's not really an important issue, but I would appreciate it if you wouldn't', rather than 'Why can't you just stop doing that? You know it drives me mad, but you just don't stop, do you?' The message is the same, but the first communication conveys a spirit of partnership and shared responsibility, whereas the second will generate antagonism, make the other person feel both defensive and angry, and far less well-disposed towards cooperating with our wishes.

Similar situations arise in a workplace environment. If a manager is asking an employee to carry out a task, how he or she chooses to convey the message is just as important as the words used.

constructive criticism versus fault-finding

The motive behind true criticism is constructive – we seek to give our friend or colleague feedback in the anticipation that our help will lead to improvement and progress. Fault-finding, on the other hand, is destructive, like grumbling. It has a negative rather than a positive motive and can therefore lead to discouragement. It can also convey a notion of superiority – we feel we are in a position to judge our friend or colleague. We draw attention to our perception of their shortcomings rather than working with them, on an equal footing, to achieve a better outcome.

Constructive criticism can be as critical as fault-finding; the distinction comes from inside, from our motive in offering criticism. We can convey our motives by drawing on the distinction that was discussed above – the importance of how we say something. If we offer our criticism in a friendly way, highlighting positive traits the person has and can use in improving what we regard as problem areas, our friend or colleague is less likely to feel threatened or discouraged. He or she will then be more likely to appreciate our help and proceed to make genuine improvement and progress.

serving others versus waiting on them

In our modern society, most of us share in the belief that equality is a goal towards which we should all strive. In an equal society, the slavish type of service common in the past is replaced by service built on dignity and mutual respect. No one, even those closest to us, has the right to demand we wait on them, but that does not mean that service should not play a part in our lives. We can serve our partner out of love, and help our friend or colleague out of respect. The important thing is that the service is done within an equal relationship, with our knowing full well that our partner or friend would return the favour out of love and respect, without our needing to ask. We shall discuss service in more detail in Chapter 6.

spirituality versus organized religion

We shall be dealing with the spiritual side of our lives, particularly prayer, contemplation and meditation, later in this book, but the distinction between spirituality and organized religion is an important one. Organized religion, 'the Church' in the Christian faith, is made by human beings, whereas spirituality, for those who believe, comes from God. For those without religious conviction, spirituality comes from a part of themselves that they cannot ever really comprehend. Whatever we believe about the source of spirituality, it refers to the part of us that is free from the earthly categories of space and time, that can manifest itself in intuition and dreams. It is a feeling that encompasses and embraces us with its warmth, strength and support.

action versus reaction

To react means to allow ourselves and our actions to be determined by others or by external circumstances; to act, in contrast, is always our own decision. Only we as individuals can decide whether to initiate something, whereas if we react, we are just responding to someone else's will. Reacting to other people or situations regularly reflects too little self-belief and an often unconscious desire to be dependent on others, to let others take the responsibility that should be ours. To act, on the other hand, involves a conscious decision on our part. Action is constructive; it enables us to remain free and independent, to control circumstances and remain masters of our lives.

Frequently one must react to others out of courtesy, but one should do so by means of action wherever possible. Imagine, for example, that you are in a gathering of people, perhaps a party or business meeting. One of the group is being deliberately difficult, disagreeing with everything and generally inhibiting the satisfactory progress of the meeting or conversation. It would be very easy for you to react angrily, criticizing their behaviour and drawing attention to their obstructiveness. This would be letting the other person call the shots – your reaction would merely demonstrate the control they are exerting. The more constructive path would be to divert the course of the conversation away from the individual in question, to change the subject or to invite someone else to give their opinion. Here you would be acting for a constructive purpose rather than further contributing to the negative tone the annoying individual is already setting. Even if you do not actually manage to intervene in a situation such as this, renouncing a negative response and considering what positive course may be open to you is already an action rather than a reaction.

self-assessment versus self-importance

Self-assessment is a necessary precondition for our personal development – we cannot establish what we seek to achieve if we have not identified our starting point. Self-assessment involves becoming aware of and being honest about both our positive and negative traits in as unbiased a way as possible. If we are not prepared to see ourselves as we really are, we will end up struggling against ourselves, wasting our energy and effort.

A certain amount of self-importance is essential to achieve self-assessment – we have to believe that we are worth the effort that getting to know ourselves and establishing our goals and priorities requires. But it is important not to be carried away by self-importance, not to develop an inflated self-opinion, as this goes directly counter to what self-assessment is intended to achieve – a realistic picture of what makes us who we are.

the community versus the individual

I have devoted a lot of space in this book to looking at people as individuals, concentrating on how we can improve our life by reinforcing belief in ourselves. But it is important to remember that as well as being self-contained individuals, we are equal citizens in a greater community, or rather communities. We are members of everything from a family, a school, and a country, to the community of the human race. It is important to distinguish when the needs of the individual, whether ourselves or others, should be predominant, and when the requirements of a larger community are more important. We shall discuss this in more detail in Chapter 8. Particularly in areas of our life such as work, justice, politics, schooling and our role in the local community, we must be aware that we play just a small part in a far bigger picture. We should take seriously the laws of the state, as well as the usually unwritten rules that enable the other communities of which we are a part to function effectively, and take care not to assume authority that goes beyond our rights as equal members of the community.

We were born to unite with our fellow men, and to join in community with the human race.

Cicero

adaptation versus conformism

Initially, this may appear to be another very subtle distinction, as both adaptation and conformism refer to our modifying our behaviour, attitude or outlook to be closer to that of others. However, just as with the distinctions between spontaneity and impulsiveness, and between criticism and fault-finding, one is a positive response, one a negative. If we conform unquestioningly to the norms of a community, whether a business, religious community or family, we are reacting rather than acting (see pp. 69–70), letting the community take the lead and moulding ourselves to it. This is another example of our renouncing responsibility for our own personal development and placing it on others. Conforming can also be dangerous as it fails to take into account the fact that communities of all types can make mistakes and develop along inappropriate paths. If people conform unquestioningly they can therefore find themselves unwittingly treading an undesirable route.

Adaptation, by contrast, is a conscious act, in which the individual adapts himself or herself in identifiable ways to fit in with a community, but does not let the community take control. The individual maintains a critical eye within the community and can help it thrive and develop, unlike the conformist who accepts the *status quo* and can therefore hinder the community's progress. Effective adaptation benefits both the individual and the community, and rather than being a short-term solution to an individual's need to belong, as conforming so often is, adaptation is a positive step both for the present and future health of the individual and society.

words versus deeds

This suggests that there is an opposition between words and deeds and all too often this is the case. But an important step in nurturing our self-belief is minimizing any mismatch between word and deed, to strive to make our words correspond to our actions and our behaviour. Otherwise our words will have no effect, even if they are correct in principle.

It can be difficult to live up to the goal of direct correspondence between word and deed, and we are often accused of hypocrisy if we cannot achieve it. Most of us can recall situations where we have been adamant in our comments that someone should act in a certain way – perhaps we have advised a friend to be more sensible with their money or to treat someone else in a particular way – only to find ourselves not following our own advice at a subsequent date. Our inability to match word and deed is reflected in the saying, 'Don't do as I do; do as I say'. But if we are truly to believe in ourselves, we must have the energy and strength to modify our behaviour. We must live our lives by the same rules as we advise others to live theirs, and not give in to the weaknesses we are all too quick to criticize in others.

There are countless other examples of fine distinctions that space does not allow us to cover here. You can probably think of some that are particularly relevant to your own experiences.

 Tip By consciously using your inner senses you can make fine distinctions and build both your own self-belief and the self-belief of others.

developing our capacity
to love

People have written about love since time immemorial,
but that does not necessarily mean that we understand
what it really is. It is probably impossible to formulate an
exact definition of love, as everyone uses the word in a different way and it conjures up different associations for
every individual. Most of us would agree, however, that it
is about selflessly giving of ourself to others, about sacrificing all we have and are, and that it involves generosity,
honesty, humility, patience, compassion and kindness.

> *Love is patient, love is kind. It does not envy, it does not
> boast, it is not proud. It is not rude, it is not self-seeking,
> it is not easily angered, it keeps no record of wrongs. Love
> does not delight in evil but rejoices with the truth. It
> always protects, always trusts, always hopes, always per-
> severes. Love never fails.*
>
> Holy Bible, I Corinthians 13:3–6

> *Our heart shall not waver; and we will abide in compas-
> sion, in loving-kindness, without resentment. We will
> think of the man who speaks ill of us with thoughts of
> love, and in our thoughts of love shall we dwell. And from*

that abode of love we will fill the whole world with far-reaching, wide-spreading, boundless love.

Majjhima Nikaya

Many of the best descriptions of love come from the sacred scriptures of the world, and all the great religious leaders spoke of the necessity of love. However, whatever one's religious beliefs, there are many different types of love, and for everyone love is an intense spiritual feeling that involves several levels. On an intimate level, if I believe, I can love God with all of myself; I can love another individual with all of my heart; on a personal level I can love a limited number of my fellow human beings; but on a spiritual level, I can love all the people on this earth, regardless of religion, race, culture or nation.

overcoming fear

Love is a light that never dwells in a heart possessed by fear.

Bahá'u'lláh

As this quotation demonstrates, fear is the major barrier to developing our capacity to love, a capacity we need if we are to promote our self-belief. Today, in our discouraging, emotional, competitive world, there are few people who can say truthfully that they are 100 per cent free of fear, be it conscious or unconscious. Most widespread are fear of others and fear of blame. What do others think of me? Do they accept me? Do they understand me? Do they disapprove of what I do or say? Will they discover how worthless I am? Fear can also be linked to gender issues – many men still feel that they must appear strong and fearless, while many women feel that, as well as being strong for themselves, they must prove their importance in the so-called 'gender war'.

Fear is an increased sense of inferiority. It can refer to fear of responsibility, of lack of success, of poverty, of illness, of the future, and more often than not refers to everything which is unknown.

In a doctor's waiting room, one woman said to another: 'I've already been feeling much better since the doctor told me that I do have something that requires treatment.'

Even though this woman has been told she is ill, she prefers this to the fear of the unknown, to the uncertainty. As this demonstrates, fear is the opposite of feeling secure.

So the question is, how can I learn to diminish my fears, to become more conscious of them so that I can work to limit their role in my life? A good first step on the path to overcoming fear is understanding where it comes from. Much of our fear derives from the fact that we often do not like to change our thinking, to think anew, or if we are willing to do this, we often find it difficult to be patient. Together with our prejudicial view that people are by nature self-centred and aggressive, we can often feel paralyzed and fearful.

The key is that fear is an emotion and, as we have already discussed, we can use our decision-making powers to avoid our emotions, including fear, from taking over our lives. We have the ability to change our attitudes very fast and so can choose both to believe that we can change our thinking and to reject the self-centred side of our nature. This process can be helped by establishing what unconscious goals we are aiming for. But probably the most vital step in moving from fear to love is to change our eyes to see more positively.

learning to love

Just as in Chapter 2 we discussed how to nurture our insight and our inner senses to improve our self-development, our capacity to love also needs constant nurturing. We must strive for perfect insight and perfect love even though we know that perfection is unachievable. Insight and love are actually quite similar; striving for the former means developing and refining our faculty of reason, whereas striving for love involves developing and refining our feelings so that they can come closer to their highest possible form. In both cases we know that we will never reach these ultimate goals, but they are always there to show us the direction in which we should be working. While aiming for perfection, we must remain realistic.

> *Knowledge makes arrogant, but love edifies.*
> Holy Bible, I Corinthians 8:2

It may initially seem ridiculous that anyone should have to learn to love. 'Surely love just comes naturally', you may be thinking. 'It's not something you can learn.' Everyone has an inborn capacity to love, but this capacity needs to be developed, which requires help from other people. You cannot learn everything to do with love, but as with most human activities, there are certain preparations you must make before it can happen. Just as when you want to swim, you have to get into the water, if you want to love, you must open your heart and mix with other people. You cannot learn to love for yourself alone.

Fortunate people learn to love from their childhood experiences. A child's parents are usually the first people to show love to a child and therefore the first to teach the child how to love. The more the parents believe in love and the more love they can give and demonstrate, the greater the chances that their child will develop a strong capacity to love. If a child is shown insufficient affection by her parents, or by whoever brings her up, either because they have not sufficiently developed their own capacity to love, or because preference was given to a brother or sister, there is a danger that the child will have a limited capacity to love when she reaches adulthood. Similarly, adults who were shown too much love in childhood, who see the excessive love of a parent as a bind, or a golden cage, can have difficulty expressing love to their own children. Such people may be fortunate enough to find loving friends or a loving partner, and will learn from them how to love, but it is quite likely that their belief in their inability to love will inhibit them from being able to establish loving friendships and relationships. They may turn the absence or excess of love back on themselves, and look inward to find reasons for the treatment they received. They may falsely conclude that it is their own fault that they cannot be loved or are incapable of loving. As a result, they will have little self-belief or sense of personal value.

loving ourselves

The vital first step in developing our capacity to love is learning to love ourselves. The relationship between believing in yourself and fear is circular – if we do not believe in ourselves, we will be full of fear, but at the same time we need to overcome our fear to believe in ourselves. How can we really expect to be able to love others, if we do not love ourselves? And if we don't perceive ourselves as worthy of love, how can we expect others to love us? Of course, by loving ourselves, we do not mean egocentric or egoistic love, but honest appreciation of our strengths and our contribution to the world.

However much you feel that your inability to love and be loved is deeply entrenched, it is perfectly possible to 'learn' how to love, as the following case demonstrates.

Eric is 41, lives alone and has neither male friends nor a girlfriend. He recently inherited a small amount of money and decided to use this to seek advice from a psychotherapist. He feels that he has been unhappy all his life; he did not do himself justice at school and does not have a career to stimulate him, surviving on casual work. He reads widely but knows perfectly well that his books are a substitute for people; he escapes into other worlds to escape the inadequacy of his own.

At the first consultation, his life history revealed that he had grown up in the shadow of an elder brother who was outstanding in every field – at home, at school, in sports and in music. He also had a younger sister, so he was the middle child. He was continually compared with both his successful brother, who was held up as a role-model, and his sister, who, with her good looks and charm, was popular with everyone and had countless friends. Soon Eric became the black sheep of the family. As a consequence, he felt unloved during his childhood and became more and more difficult. This prompted his failure at school, and his parents became even more ashamed of him, while his brother and sister grew in their estimation.

To escape, Eric left home young and severed all contact with his family. He frequently contemplated suicide because he considered his life to be a complete mess. He felt deeply unloved and thought that happiness would elude him throughout his life.

Fortunately, the psychotherapist was able to gain Eric's trust, although this was not easy as Eric's feelings of discouragement were initially very high. Together they worked through the fact that Eric's behaviour had always hindered the satisfaction of his lifelong longing for love. Slowly Eric has begun to regain his faith in himself and to accept that love can be learned. Very gradually he has started to see people with different eyes and to accept that they probably do not perceive him in the way he anticipates.

Although this life history is quite extreme, features of Eric's case appear in many of our lives. Just like Eric, the most important thing to do is change your opinion of yourself. All individuals, including you, are unbelievably rich in the potential they can fulfil.

One way of developing self-love, and confirming your rich potential, without the expert help of a psychologist, is to take a piece of paper and write down on the left all the things you find positive in yourself and on the right all the negative things. Be as spontaneous and objective as possible. Do not worry about feeling that you are being vain – you are not – this is all about positive self-evaluation. You should also not expect to judge yourself in an entirely positive way – if you did, you would not be being objective. You will of course be happy with your list of positive things, but rather than get down about the negative ones, you can start to decrease them. You may not feel this is possible, but you know you can do it because you have learned to believe in your power of making conscious decisions. To reinforce this, you can even check what you have removed from your negative list and added to your positive one every week, or even every day. You can add the opposite of most things you delete from your negative list, perhaps 'intolerance' for example, to your positive one. Allied to this, you should never forget the importance of retaining what I call 'positive eyes'. After someone has decided for themselves that negative things cannot exist, they become only the absence of positive things, and therefore less threatening to self-belief.

Other important strategies to concentrate on to improve your love of yourself and thereby your self-belief, are to forget the past with all its feelings of guilt, taking from it only what is useful for your future behaviour. Similarly, you must remember that far more important than facts is how we use them. Keeping your 'positive eyes' open will help you forget words like 'difficult' and 'must'. You must concentrate on the good in your life – perhaps you have friends who love you, perhaps a partner with whom you share your life, a job that takes financial pressure off you, or gives you the intellectual stimulation you need. You can always do better, but it is important not to be ambitious in an exaggerated way. You do not need to be better than others. Your life is okay; it is balanced without being the best. You are not, and will never be perfect, but you are worthy of your own love.

loving each other

As we have discussed, we are social beings; we cannot exist in isolation. We live in a community, and are dependent on it for most of what we need, from food and clothes to language. Everyone is born with a sense of community, but as with our ability to love, this can only reveal itself if it is consciously developed. Our sense of community and our ability to love are strongly linked; a sense of community is faith in others, love for one's fellow human beings.

The greater the sense of community, the more love becomes the means for making the greatest contribution to others and the most honest expression of the sense of belonging.
Rudolf Dreikurs

Dreikurs also believed that only courageous people are capable of experiencing real love. Without trust in ourselves and others, constructive love is impossible.

Trust and respect are the two inseparable cornerstones of love, without which it cannot exist.

Kleist

We experience many contexts in which we have to love others throughout our lives – in our families, playgroup, school, college, work, as we pursue our leisure activities, even just on the street – and we can always learn how to love others better.

We shall not discuss family love in detail here as it is different from most other kinds of love that are to do with relationships outside the family. Family members who live together, while they still have to concentrate on nurturing positive relationships, are by their physical proximity, given a certain sort of headstart in building relationships. But family life is often decisive in establishing how we build up loving relationships in our adult lives.

Julia is 27 years old and has a successful professional career. She lives alone but has plenty of friends. She is an only child, and was brought up by parents who fought on a regular basis. Her mother had a busy job and seemed to have insufficient time for her daughter. Her father had time for her, but was a harsh man, and often beat her. Sometimes he treated her nicely, but never for very long. Mostly he shouted at her and threatened her. She did not dare discuss what was happening to her with anyone.

Julia was successful academically, and in her later school life went away to boarding school, and did not go home even in the holidays. After a few years her parents divorced and lived a long way apart. Julia finished her studies and found a good job that more than adequately provides for her financially.

Although she had a successful social life, she knew her life was troubled by her past, so went to see a therapist. The therapist advised her to visit her parents, whom she had not seen for many years. With the therapist's help and support, she learned to understand that much of her troubles were to do with her reacting to the behaviour of her parents, and that this need not be the case. It was in her power to decide the outcome of the situation, and she could choose that she need not imitate their behaviour. When she did go to visit them, she realized that she was the only one who had changed. Although both parents were glad at her visit, they did not show it. But Julia was able to look at them with very different eyes and decided to visit them again.

With the help of the therapist, and drawing on her own renewed sense of self-belief and her belief in her ability consciously to decide on her actions, Julia was able to overcome her past and start to love other people with a positive outlook. She renewed relationships not only with the people who had caused her so much pain in her childhood, but she also found her other relationships improved by her change of heart, by her looking with positive rather than negative eyes.

countering discouragement

In Chapter 1 we explored how discouragement makes us egocentric, pushing us towards obsession as we compare ourselves to others out of fear and self-doubt. The fact that we live in a discouraging society is a major obstacle to the development of love – if we are constantly looking inwards, we cannot send our love outwards. We must not allow ourselves to yield to the temptation to use discouragement as an excuse. We must consciously switch from discouragement to encouragement, to help turn major fears into minor ones, and help reduce fear and increase love.

Robert was so discouraged that he was never able to approach people. If people did not approach him, he would never have had any friends. He was admired for his appearance, but his withdrawn nature was due to more than shyness; he genuinely believed he had nothing to offer anybody. One day he met a couple who were far older than him in a wine bar. They were on the next table to Robert, and the man immediately started talking to him, making jokes and discussing interesting issues. When Robert was about to leave, his new friend asked him to stay a little longer, and when Robert did finally go, the couple said they would very much like to see him again. Robert first hesitated, as he could not believe that such warm people would be interested in him, but he agreed, happily.

That evening was the beginning of a deep and long friendship. The couple and Robert gave each other far more than they were aware. Robert's new friends introduced him to others, who responded equally well to Robert's reserve, and he slowly gained more confidence. He gradually learned to initiate rather than just respond when it came to conversations with others, and also began to develop friendships with people his own age. Now he is in a successful relationship; the first time a woman has returned his affection.

In the past three case histories we have looked at, Robert, Julia and Eric were severely discouraged in their relationships with others. Their examples show, however, that, using a combination of our conscious decision-making powers and creating opportunities when they are presented to us, we can all reduce our feelings of discouragement and fear, and build up our capacity to love, both ourselves and others.

Love is a mutual self-giving which ends in self-recovery.
Fulton J. Sheen

There is no fear in love; but perfect love casts out fear.
Holy Bible, I John 4:18

 Tip **Love is the food on which self-belief feeds.**

5 lessening our readiness for conflict

the need to be right

Every conflict in the world starts in the same way – one person who thinks they are right encounters another who is equally convinced they are right, and neither party is willing to concede the merits of the other's case. This principle applies equally to conflicts between individuals and groups, whether the conflict is between partners or business colleagues, between factions in families or between nations.

The phenomenon may be observed everywhere – at home, at school, at work and in particular in business and politics – but where does it come from? What makes us so willing to participate in confrontation with our fellow human beings, rather than be able to put a requirement for harmony before our need to be right?

Much of the problem revolves around our upbringing. It is inevitable, and important, that parents emphasize what is good and virtuous to their children, so that they can grow up with a sound moral code with which to make their own decisions about life. But parents can overstress to children how important being right is, sometimes rank-ing 'rightness' higher than individuals themselves. This can mean that we grow up attributing value to individuals according to whether they are right or not, 'rightness' being regarded as superior, 'wrongness' inferior. Inside, we know that the value of individuals has nothing to do with them being right or not; we are all equal human beings and 'rightness' or 'wrongness' has nothing to do with it. Furthermore, it is impossible to be right all the time – peo-ple who expect this of themselves are being unrealistic and are doomed to disappointment. In addition, a person who always tries to be right gets on everybody else's nerves! But however much we may accept that rightness is not absolute – that what could be described as a 'both–and' approach is both more sensible and fairer – there is no escaping from the fact that people do not like to be considered inferior. They try to identify themselves with what they believe to be 'right' in order to gain a sense of their own superiority. Being right makes it easier to obtain a sense of our own worth; it makes us feel stronger because we live in a competitive society where, as we discussed in Chapter 4, the threat of discourage-ment is always strong.

> *Extremity of right is wrong.*
>
> John Clarke

Although being right may make it easier for us to have faith in ourselves, participation in conflict, the drive to prove our rightness, and in so doing to prove someone else wrong, are tell-tale signs of a lack of self-belief. If some-one wants to prove to me that I am wrong, despite their assertions of 'rightness', I know that they are behaving in this way because they have too little self-belief and are therefore trying to demonstrate the superiority they aspire to. If individuals really believe in themselves, they do not need to assert their superiority over others, but can discuss areas of difference in a context of equality. They will be less interested in arguing about who is right, and more motivated to explore common ground. In this chapter, we shall be discussing different types of conflict and how they can be amicably resolved, to help you reinforce your sense of self-belief and thereby lessen your readiness for conflict.

types of conflict

Although, as we have discussed, all conflict stems from disagreement over what constitutes right and wrong, it is possible to identify different types of conflicts. It can be helpful to know what has caused the conflict in order to establish how best to resolve it. We shall be exploring how conflicts can be resolved on pp. 93–8 of this book; first we will look at the most common types of conflict.

conflict about beliefs or ideas

A frequent cause of conflict between individuals, families and larger communities, involves disagreement over ideas, rights or beliefs. As we discussed on pp. 60–1, we are very prone to giving our opinions or experience the status of 'facts', making them unquestionably 'right' as far as we are concerned, and we therefore become unwilling to compromise them in the face of opposition.

On a global level, for example, this can lead to conflict over national boundaries, threatening the peaceful coexistence of different peoples; over religion, as one religious community seeks to assert its 'rightness' over another; or over political freedom, as one party strives to achieve dominance. But in situations like this, people should have the self-belief to accept 'otherness' without fearing that it threatens their own belief system. The social equality of all people should predominate, irrespective of differences of race, religion, culture, skin-colour, sex or age. All people have certain fundamental rights, such as the right to peace, privacy, personal liberty, freedom of thought, conscience and religion. They all have the right to develop their spiritual faculties freely, including justice, love, empathy, compassion, trustworthiness, honesty and a sense of community. They have the right to work, to have decent living conditions and to pursue happiness, education, culture, insight, responsibility, a meaningful existence, to contribute their achievements to humanity. None of us has the right to threaten any one of these rights, however strongly held our beliefs may be.

On a more local scale, we must respect the various rights accorded to individuals in a community on the basis of their different functions or life patterns. In the family community, for example, if a mother goes out to work but comes home for lunch, the limitations of her life style give her the right to determine the time of the meal, as her work commitments constrain her choices on when and for how long she can come home. However much a child in the house believes it is his right to postpone the meal time so that he can finish building a tower of bricks, he has to accept that it is appropriate that his parent's requirements should take precedence over his desires, and not turn the issue into a cause of conflict.

It is important that we learn at a young age that we must not put what we regard as our rights or beliefs in competition with the rights of others. Parents can use the situations of conflict that inevitably develop in childhood to teach their children how to respect the beliefs of others and strive to avoid conflict.

Karen, a young mother, found her three-year-old twin daughters engaged in a bitter argument:

'I'm me, and you're you', screamed one.

'No', screamed the other back, 'I'm me, and you're you!'

How was she to resolve this seeming irreconcilable difference, particularly when it was all she could do not to laugh?

Both the twins were right, but each one saw only their own point of view; neither was able to see the whole, and neither of them was able to accommodate the other's position. It would not have been possible for Karen to persuade either one of the children to change their mind – after all, they were both right – and it is good to encourage children to form their own opinions. But although it was not surprising that Karen's main response to the situation was humour, she should have used the incident to explain to her children that love and respect for others is more important than being right.

This example also demonstrates that nothing is too trivial to become the subject of a quarrel. Conflicts frequently develop because an issue is regarded as very serious by one party and so trivial by the other that they refuse to discuss it. But it is important to remember that we must respect the equality of the other person and accept our mutual responsibility, so if something is important to the other person, it should be important to us.

We can also experience conflict born of difference of ideas in our closest relationships, as in the following example.

Peter and Sally Kay have been married for almost a year and have lately been having more and more rows about housework. Both of them have full-time jobs, but Peter expects Sally to do the housework in the evenings, helping only occasionally. Sally has the strong impression that he does so out of condescension, and that he only pays lip-service to the idea of the equality of men and women. In reality, like many men, he had developed the idea that housework was something inferior during his childhood, when his parents assumed traditional gender roles. Sally sought advice from a friend, who recommended talking openly with her husband. So Sally plucked up the courage to ask her husband to discuss the situation with her. He agreed, and they had a very important series of conversations in which they shared experiences they remembered from their childhood, and discussed their own and their parents' attitudes on what household tasks should be performed by husband and wife. Although Peter was sensitive about Sally's implicit criticism of his attitude, they were able to have a cool, equal discussion and agree a way of getting the domestic chores done that involved both of them equally.

In this scenario, as Sally and Peter were not only sensible but also held each other in great affection, they were able, in the course of their several conversations, to understand their own ideas and those of their partner better. Rather than use the issue of their different opinions to generate conflict, together they were able to draw relevant conclusions and reach practical compromises for their married life.

Whether on a global, local or intimate personal level, there are similar lessons to be learned about how to avoid or deal with conflict caused by differences of ideas or opinions:

- remember that what you believe to be right may only be right to you and you must respect others' difference of opinion
- whatever you may believe, you must not infringe on the basic rights of your fellow human beings,

and must accept and respect your role in being responsible for them

- while being true to yourself, you should believe in yourself sufficiently to know when someone else's case is stronger than yours and back down graciously
- if something is important to someone else, however trivial it may seem to you, respect their opinion and take it seriously out of love and respect for them.

conflict over emotions

Perhaps the most common factors leading to conflict and disunity are our emotions. As we have already discussed, emotions, if not controlled, can threaten our life in human society. Conflict between individuals caused by a clash of emotions can be even more difficult to manage than one caused by a difference of beliefs or ideas, as the dominance of emotion means that both parties are too far removed from their decision-making faculty to be able to respond in a considered manner.

> Martin's young daughter has been behaving badly and Martin is getting more and more annoyed. As usual, he tries to deal with the problem on an equal level, and asks his daughter, 'Why did you do that?' As with many young children, he receives the answer, 'I don't know.' This annoys Martin even more, and he loses his patience and snaps at his daughter, who promptly starts to cry.

In this situation, although Martin started with good intentions, the situation has become one of emotional conflict; frustration mixed with anger on Martin's part and distress on the part of his daughter. Martin should have realized that in many cases children really do not know why they are misbehaving. He could have worked out that his daughter's bad behaviour represented her working towards an unconscious goal of grabbing her father's attention. If Martin had understood this, he would have realized that his anger or annoyance would achieve nothing. He could have considered why his daughter felt the need to summon his attention in a way that was bound to produce a negative result, and reflected on how he could behave towards his daughter in future so that she would not feel the need to draw negative attention to herself.

This case demonstrates how effective conflict resolution frequently involves assessing what goal the other party is trying to achieve by means of their behaviour, and addressing it, rather than reacting impulsively to the individual's surface behaviour. We will be dealing with this more fully in the next section.

Conflict is particularly hard to resolve when it is initiated by an unpremeditated and unexpected attack, as frequently occurs when confrontation is prompted by emotional difference. Perhaps someone suddenly becomes angry and snaps at us, or something happens to push someone who is already distressed too far, and they burst into tears. If I am attacked by an angry person, the urge to defend myself and justify my opinion will be even stronger than if I feel threatened by a calmer, more respectful person. It is important that we do not let such situations lead to conflict, but try and let an equal, matter-of-fact discussion ensue, avoiding the otherwise inevitable consequence of both parties feeling threatened and bitter. We should ensure that self-justification does not turn into a counter-attack, but that we assert our opinion in a loving, objective way, without the aim of achieving superiority over the other person. If both of us achieve this, the discussion can lead us both to new insights and reinforced self-belief rather than leaving either or both of us feeling threatened.

Of all the emotions that can spark conflict, jealousy is a real love-killer, arguably the most dangerous. As an emotion that is profoundly felt, it can be extremely difficult to be objective about, and can therefore provoke long-term conflict. The jealous party, irrespective of whether the jealousy is justified or not, inevitably feels that all the ill has been done to him or her, and will refuse to accept that the jealousy is a powerful means of determining the other person – a means of pursuing goal 3, a sense of superiority. The non-jealous party feels helpless and defenceless, and is unable to find any satisfactory means of putting his or her friend's mind at rest.

This kind of conflict is a prime example of a conflict born of inappropriate distinction between facts and experience – the jealous partner perceives a fact, the other does not. The only way this conflict will begin to be resolved is for both parties, particularly the jealous one, to acknowledge this distinction, and the strength of the bond between them, before any feelings of pride or hurt.

the principles of conflict resolution

Many people do not really know how to solve conflicts and end up either applying a principle of trial and error to see what works, or resolutely sticking to 'their way of doing things' regardless of the outcome. Many people decide to 'sleep on it' and resolve the conflict with a new, positive approach the following morning when they have calmed down and their heads are clearer. But it often happens that the differences seem to have grown of their own accord during the night, particularly as the people involved will have gone to sleep thinking about the issues that separate them, so the conflict will often be continued with renewed energy. Others try not talking to each other for a while, waiting for the mutual antipathy to disappear by itself. This may be feasible too, but it is just as likely that, during the period of silence, the antipathy will build up rather than fade away, risking a prolonging of the conflict rather than a resolution of it. The worst situation is that of the couple who fight at night until one or both of them are so exhausted that they fall asleep without having resolved their differences. The next morning they go about their daily tasks feeling tired, washed out, despondent and morose, only to start up the conflict again at the next opportunity, their tiredness contributing to sustaining the emotional tension and prolonging the conflict.

Successful conflict resolution requires knowledge of five simple steps that can be applied to all types of conflict.

---

five steps to successful conflict resolution

1. adopt the right attitude

2. maintain mutual respect

3. think what the other person's goals might be

4. reach a conscious, constructive agreement

5. accept your responsibility

Step 1   It is essential to adopt the right attitude. This involves being right-minded in three ways. First, I must accept the situation. I must see the conflict, and particularly its resolution, as an opportunity to gain something positive both for myself and for my relationship with the other person, and I must look forward to our both sharing the sun after the storm. Second, I must appreciate that I can decide consciously to influence and change my mood, my disappointment or dissatisfaction, the inevitable side-effects of conflict. Third, I must forget my feelings of powerlessness and my desire for prestige or superiority, and remind myself that actions speak louder than words – I must not only think about what I should say, but also what I should do.

Step 2   Nothing can be achieved without mutual respect. I must separate my 'opponent' himself from his behaviour, so that I see him in a positive light even if I reject what he does – I should distinguish between the doer and the deed (see pp. 62–4). I must also remember the fine distinction between arguing and surrendering, on the one hand, and understanding and helping, on the other (see p. 55), reminding myself that neither arguing nor surrendering are useful, and that understanding and helping the other person is all that is needed in order to make progress. Rather than criticize the other person, I should ask myself, 'What have I done wrong in this conflict? Was I seeking to be right or to justify myself? How have I discouraged my friend? Was I seeking to dominate him – did I try and tell him what to do and what not to do?'

Step 3   As we have mentioned before, I should consider the motives, or goals, each of us was pursuing when the conflict broke out.

Step 4   It is important that the two of us reach a conscious agreement to end the conflict, that we both desire the same outcome – to build the future in a constructive way. In addition to the obvious subject of the conflict – the issue we are raising our voices about – we should examine the context behind our disagreement. Had the past or some particular fact taken on too great a significance for us that we are taking it out on each other? Is our conflict really about the subject we think it is?

Step 5   Nothing, particularly conflict resolution, can take place in the absence of cooperation. We must both take a share of the responsibility for the disagreement and for its resolution. I should ask myself what I can change in myself, and consider the questions, 'What can I do?' and 'Did I have too little courage to accept that I am not always right?'.

applying the principles

> Ed and Kelly frequently find themselves in conflict with one another. Ed would be the first to admit that he is not particularly tidy. This is in total contrast to Kelly, who would like their home to be spick and span at all times. Today the weather is awful – it has been snowing recently, but most of the snow has melted and there is sludge everywhere. Kelly is in the entrance hall when her husband walks in. As usual he does not wipe his feet properly and leaves dirty marks on the floor. In a spirit of love, Kelly asks him nicely to go back and clean his shoes more thoroughly because of the terrible weather. He good-naturedly returns to the doormat and does what she asks. But the next day the same thing happens again. Kelly is a little more annoyed this time, but Ed apologizes, gives her a hug, and promises to remember next time. Next time, however, he forgets yet again and Kelly cannot hold back but shouts at him angrily. He becomes angry at her complaint so defends himself by criticizing something she regularly does. The evening is ruined.

Step 1 This case demonstrates, as did the example of Martin and his daughter earlier in the chapter, that anger gets us nowhere. Although Kelly starts off in a 'spirit of love', her anger definitely shows the wrong rather than the right attitude. Similarly, the fact that Ed did not wipe his feet in the first instance would indicate a lack of respect for the importance his wife attributes to tidiness in the home. This is reinforced by his forgetting to do it a second time. Rather than see the conflict as an opportunity to meet each other halfway and attain a better mutual understanding, both Ed and Kelly are sticking remorselessly to their own positions. Each sees the other as being responsible for the conflict and the dissatisfaction that they feel, rather than accepting their own power to modify their feelings and attitudes. They should both reject their anger, and try and resolve the problem with an attitude of optimism and loving calm.

Step 2   Both Ed and Kelly are guilty of having insufficient respect for each other. Ed's disrespect is more blatant, but Kelly shows little respect for her husband's feelings when she shouts at him. Both of them need to separate the doer from the deed, and concentrate on the strength of the relationship between them rather than on the deeds each has done that annoy the other. Rather than focusing on each other, concentrating on each other's contribution to the conflict, they should examine themselves – Ed could ask himself why he has continued to pursue a mode of behaviour he knows will irritate his wife; Kelly could ask herself why this one piece of behaviour annoys her so much and whether there is anything she can do to tackle it herself.

Step 3   When Kelly became angry for the first time – understandable though her annoyance was – she was unconsciously pursuing goal 2, for care and attention. She received loving attention from her husband so was satisfied for the moment. The next time, however, her goal was to obtain a feeling of superiority over her husband – goal 3. She was basking in the glory of her superior tidiness. Her husband felt threatened by this, did not want to feel inferior, so open conflict ensued. Had Kelly continued to show her annoyance the next day, she would have been aiming for goal 4, striving for revenge, to punish Ed for his repeated misdemeanour.

What about Ed? Like his wife, his persistent refusal to wipe his feet, knowingly against Kelly's wishes, demonstrates he was also working towards goal 3, superiority, or at least an absence of inferiority.

To summarize, Kelly was seeking, through her tidiness, to be dominant in the home, whilst Ed put up resistance by means of his disregard for her viewpoint. It is not important which came first, as both Kelly and Ed were obviously very well prepared for this game of conflict. Both were striving for superiority; they could probably see this in each other, but not in themselves. As with prejudice, it is much easier to recognize the immediate goals being pursued by another person rather than the ones you are aiming for yourself.

Learning to recognize your immediate goals is an important skill which most people do not have, but which we should all strive for. If I consider which of the five immediate goals is currently in play, then I have the opportunity not to continue to develop the emotions that are arising within me, but to make a conscious decision about whether or not to continue to pursue the goal I have identified. As this goal will be negative, and since, like everyone else, I want to have a good opinion of myself, I am unlikely to pursue the goal further with a clear conscience, and this is an important step towards resolving conflict. If both parties can achieve this, it is far more likely that any conflict will be resolved.

Steps 4 and 5 The main reason Kelly and Ed did not manage to resolve their disagreement promptly is because they had not agreed, either with themselves or with each other, that they wanted the conflict to be over. As part of their goal of superiority, neither of them were willing to back down. To use an analogy from gardening, if the conflict was a weed, rather than pull it up by the roots, they simply snapped off its leaves, allowing it to sprout new growth. As soon as they really want the conflict to be over and are willing to look to themselves and their responsibility, they will be able to stop bickering, and start to resolve their differences sensibly.

the principles of consultation

Once we have learned to talk to rather than at one another (see pp. 65–6), we can move on to true consultation. Consultation is also about talking to one another, but that is only part of it. True consultation requires a deeper attitude of mind – it means cooperating, sharing thoughts, building a bridge between minds. It involves recognizing that everyone has something both to contribute and to learn, and that four (or more) eyes are better than two. Consultation is perhaps the highest and most spiritual of all human relationships, the cornerstone of positive living in any kind of community, particularly in the family, and is a crucial instrument for living in society, however many people are involved.

The main requirements for participants in consultation are courage, a sense of community, a mutual positive attitude, spirituality, calmness and, in particular, modesty, humility, patience, courtesy, dignity, care and moderation. A particularly essential prerequisite is a belief in equality; in other words, we need to make a conscious effort to ensure the equal status of the other participant, or participants, in the consultation process. Consultation, regardless of the subject under discussion, can only be truly successful if personal views are expressed, so no one should feel inhibited about saying what they really think. At the same time, it is worth taking care not to lay bare your soul in front of others unless you are certain that this is appropriate. It may be so in the context of a group therapy session, but it is less effective in informal consultation sessions, where it can come across as a confession and will not generally assist in finding solutions to problems. It is crucial that each participant feels happy to voice his or her opinion in complete freedom without fear of criticism, and it is important that everyone involved actively encourages this, seeking and creating opportunities to do so. No one should offend another person or feel offended if his or her opinion is contradicted – we should welcome differences of opinion because they help us to make progress. We should offer our opinions not as statements of fact but as contributions, keeping our minds open to the complexity of the issue.

Another key factor to the success of consultation is that all participants must accept that the goal is to reach a consensus – an agreement over ideas or the subsequent joint steps to be taken. Consultation can provide insight, even certainty, but it must be embarked upon with an honest striving for understanding.

Meet together, speak together,
let your minds be of one accord,
as the Gods of old, being of one mind,
accepted their share of the sacrifice.

May your counsel be common, your assembly common,
common the mind, and the thoughts of these united.
A common purpose do I lay before you,
and worship with your common obligation.

Let your aims be common,
and your hearts of one accord,
and all of you be of one mind,
so you may live well together.

Rig Veda

It is also important to remember that it is better to be unified in a wrong decision than to be in the right but have disunity. Disunity can lead to error as all participants are not working towards the same goal, whereas unity, even if a decision is wrong, can help the truth come to light more quickly, so that the decision can be corrected. If the consultation is taking place in a large group, and differences of opinion cannot be overcome, it may be that a decision can be taken by majority vote. Those who are in the minority must accept the decision for the time being, but a follow-up consultation session could be arranged so that the decision can be reviewed.

Consultation sessions can be impromptu, occurring at a convenient time that simply arises, but particularly if the subject is going to be difficult, a specific time can be arranged. There are a number of useful tips that can help the consultation run smoothly:

1. Choose the right time   All participants should agree on a suitable time for the discussion, a time when no one is troubled and can give the issue their full attention.

2. Choose the right place   You should choose somewhere you are not going to interrupted, particularly by a telephone or by visitors, and somewhere where no one is going to feel at a disadvantage.

3. Choose the right mood   If all the participants are not in a good mood, if everyone's heart is not in it, you are not going to achieve the agreement you are hoping for. You must also have the good sense to put off the discussion if anyone starts to get in a bad mood – the consultation is only going to work if everyone cooperates fully and stays focused on the issues.

4. Have pure motives   As long as everyone has absolute sincerity and goodwill, you will achieve mutual trust, with no one taking offence. All the participants will then be able to concentrate on discussing the issues rather than defending their own position. No one must use consultation to further their own interests or improve their position. If you try and score points off someone else, they will just feel challenged or accused, and will be so busy being defensive that they will be unable to discuss the issues objectively.

an example of consultation – the family council

Consultation is important for any relationship and for groups of any size. The family council, for example, is a specific case that demonstrates the merits of consultation. The family council is an unrivalled opportunity for decision-making and problem-solving, a forum for solving particular problems or discussing holiday plans, choice of school, moving house, sibling rivalry or family problems; anything that involves more than one member of the family.

The primary value of the family council is that it carries the authority of the group rather than just that of the parents. All decisions the council makes are a matter of participation, not compliance with the wishes of one or two dominant people. This can be particularly helpful when making decisions that involve teenagers, for example. Adolescent children from the ages of about fourteen or fifteen rarely respect their parents, but they often find it easier to recognize the authority of the group and to respect its advice. Everyone benefits from the family council – all members of the family learn how to think and how to take sensible decisions, even if these decisions go against their own inclinations; everyone gains a deeper understanding of each other and of themselves.

Family councils are particularly beneficial for children as they give them a positive opportunity to participate in the family on a new level. They learn that it is not wrong to express their own opinion, that they can speak out freely and say what is on their minds, and that through sharing different viewpoints, a better decision can usually be reached. It is a good idea for children to take the role of chairperson, as this will teach them the importance of maintaining order in a meeting, and of encouraging everyone to voice their opinion.

Tips

Remember your opinion is just that – an opinion, not a fact.

Having love and respect for the person you are talking to is more important than being 'right'.

Have the self-belief to back down when you sense your position is weak.

Remember the five steps to successful conflict resolution.

suffering, sacrifice and service

For those who do not believe in themselves, everything that goes wrong just serves to justify their negative self-image. Even the smallest, superficially unimportant occurrences, like joining the wrong queue in the supermarket, let alone major drawbacks like falling ill or suffering a major crisis, just seem to prove that the world is against them, that they do not merit good fortune in their lives. The key purpose of this chapter is to turn such a view around; to show that our suffering and misfortune should not be seen as reflections of low personal value, but as challenges from which we can learn both practically and spiritually, and develop renewed belief in ourselves.

the purpose of suffering

What is suffering?

> *Suffering is the fastest horse toward perfection.*
>> Traditional saying from Java

> *Suffering can serve [as] liberation from the tasks of life.*
>> Alfred Adler

To raise the enjoyment of life, sufferings intensify susceptibility.

Friedrich von Schiller

Whatever our viewpoint, few of us would dispute that suffering is the opposite of happiness and enjoyment, the converse of practical joy and spiritual fulfilment. Suffering has meant different things through the development of human history. In some cultures, people have tried to defeat suffering by means of magic; they have have not sought a purpose in suffering but have either fought against it or surrendered to it. In other cultures, people have used prayer and sacrifice to attempt to gain the favour of the god they believe has sent the suffering in the hope that he would show mercy and not send any more.

The viewpoint on suffering expressed by the major religious traditions of the world varies widely. Buddhism, for example, seeks liberation through understanding the causes of one's suffering. Christianity perceives suffering as a consequence of original sin. Another view is that suffering is the result of personal guilt – as one Jainist sutra states, 'Know that all distress arises from evil deeds'.

Whatever one's view of suffering, its causes are inevitably in the past, where they are untouchable and unchangeable. As we saw on p. 25, the only value in the past is to take from it lessons that we can consciously apply to the future. As with most events in our lives, we have the ability to decide consciously how to behave in certain circumstances, how to feel in certain situations, and suffering is no exception. We can decide our attitudes and reactions to it; we can determine the significance and effect of the suffering. A poignant example of this concerns terminal illness – something that springs to mind fairly quickly when one contemplates forms of suffering. While there is no doubt that the news that one is terminally ill would be the very worst news anyone could receive, the different ways in which the terminally ill pursue their lives shows how powerful attitude can be. Some feel that fighting the illness is not appropriate as the outcome is inevitable; others, while still distressed, seize the opportunity to do things they may have postponed for years. However bad our suffering may be, we can try to find a blessing within it, an impetus for our personal development, an advantage of some form either to ourselves or others. After all, many famous people have achieved their goals despite, or even, ironically, because of, a weakness or disorder they have. One only needs to hear of the Danish theologian and philosopher Kierkegaard, who suffered from a fatal illness; Beethoven, who continued to compose inspiring music whilst losing his hearing; Helen Keller, who wrote books and campaigned for the blind although deaf and blind herself, to recognize the role that attitude can play in turning adversity to advantage. Lord Byron, Cyrano de Bergerac, Homer, even Moses, are further examples. As Meister Eckhart stated, suffering can be 'the fastest horse for carrying a person to perfection'.

Mike ran his own business selling shop fittings, so spent most of his time driving in built-up urban streets as he made his way from customer to customer. Although he occasionally got stuck in traffic jams, which annoyed him, he was a cool driver and rarely lost his temper. One day he was travelling along a road that was usually quite busy, but, probably because he was going along it early in the morning, was on that day relatively quiet. However, he drove slowly anyway because of the speed limit. Suddenly a car appeared in his rear-view mirror, its headlights flashing and its horn hooting. The driver was obviously infuriated at Mike's slow speed and irritated that he could not overtake. Mike carried on going at the speed limit, and, as there continued to be no opportunity for the car behind to overtake, the driver kept on flashing and hooting. Eventually he managed to overtake and did so with much screeching. But rather than continue he slammed on his brakes in front of Mike's car forcing him to stop. The driver got out of the car and walked towards Mike's car. Mike wound down the window to talk to the driver – something, in hindsight, he would not have done. The man was not interested in talking – as soon as the window was wound down far enough, he thrust his fist through the open space and punched Mike vigorously and repeatedly. Held in as he was by his seat belt, Mike could do nothing. He was powerless until someone else came up and pulled the man off. Mike was seriously injured, and also at a loss about how to respond emotionally, what to make of what had happened to him. What had he done to deserve this? Could he have behaved differently? He just felt that the world was against him, that despite his efforts to lead a good life, even to the detail of obeying the speed limit, there was something about him that kept good fortune away. Where could he go from here?

Although Mike's circumstances of suffering were extreme, the feelings he experienced afterwards are quite common for those who have suffered what they perceive as totally unjust adversity. Where can they find an explanation? Who can they blame? But as I have said, Mike should try not to focus on causes and explanations, but on the future. In his heart, he knows he has done nothing wrong and rather than doubt himself he should draw strength from the fact that he stuck to his principles. He did not feel the need to accelerate, despite feeling naturally threatened by the driver's behaviour behind him, and throughout the incident did absolutely nothing wrong. Rather than allowing the experience to strengthen his self-doubt he should view it as evidence of great inner strength and use it as a foundation to build up a more positive image of himself.

Like Mike, we must use our suffering to positive advantage rather than allow it to become a weight, pushing down on us. We should let suffering be a stimulus, a ladder, a means of climbing both practically and spiritually, to a place of greater inner strength, and feel our sense of self-belief renewed through having made the climb.

Suffering is the substance of life and the root of personality, for it is only suffering that makes us persons.
Miguel de Unamuno

suffering and sacrifice

The close relationship between suffering and sacrifice has a long history. As we discussed earlier in this chapter, people often offered sacrifices to deities to appease their anger in the hope that earthly suffering would cease. For Christians, the ultimate suffering was made by Jesus Christ, who sacrificed himself so that others would be forgiven. In our daily lives, such drastic sacrifice does not play a part, but sacrifice in general terms is an important aspect of spiritualization, particularly where it concerns suffering.

So what is sacrifice? As with Jesus' sacrifice, it is the 'giving' of something from which a good will grow, just as a seed sacrifices itself so that a tree can grow, or a caterpillar sacrifices itself so that a beautiful butterfly can flourish. For ourselves, we talk about self-sacrifice, of sacrificing a part of ourselves for a greater good either for ourselves or for others. We can sacrifice in practical terms for the good of others. Examples of this include giving blood, or giving our time to a friend in need. Or we can sacrifice spiritually, as Mike needed to do. The sacrifice of his pain, his sense of victimization, would have led him to renewed self-belief. We can also sacrifice spiritually by giving up something that we enjoy, such as eating. This is why a period of fasting is a feature of so many of the religious traditions of the world. Even those of us who do not have a strong religious faith give things up, perhaps coffee or cake, because we feel there is a greater benefit to be achieved.

The ability to sacrifice and generate new birth, like the phoenix rising from the ashes, is an important step on the path of spiritualization, from egocentricity to self-belief. By sacrificing we give meaning to life; we make of adversity something new and positive. Try to think about difficult times in your life in which you felt adversity challenged your self-belief and rather than concentrating on how you felt threatened, concentrate on how you used, or could now use, what happened to you to regenerate your self-belief. To help you focus your mind on a positive view of life, when a negative one seems to want to take over, you could practise prayer and meditation, the subject of the next chapter.

the nature of true service

Service is an important step along the path of spiritualization; it is a rejection of egocentricity, as we put others before ourselves. Service is a special form of sacrifice – we sacrifice our time and effort for the benefit of others and in so doing we strengthen our self-belief. However bad we may feel about ourselves, we know that we can always do a service for, and bring benefit to, our fellow human beings, no matter how big or small the service may be.

The best of men are those who are useful to others.
Hadith of Bukhari

Historically, the word 'service' has had connotations of inequality, of 'superiors' being served by 'inferiors'. But that is an abuse of the idea of service, and, in our age of at least theoretical equality, it is a view that may at last be changing. True service has absolutely nothing to do with superiority and inferiority, and everything to do with equality, fellowship and unselfishness.

Our society would not function without service – we all depend upon others serving us and vice-versa. From its conception, the embryo is served by the mother's body; parents and teachers then serve and support the growing child; as adults we work and make our small contribution to the elaborate web of service relationships that enable human society to function. Rather than see our occupation as benefiting just ourselves, our customers and/or company, we should try and be motivated by service in our everyday work. And throughout, we should ensure that we make no value judgements about service relationships within that web. Just as it says in the Bible, all parts of the body, however small, are crucial to its working effectively. It is not possible to say which bits are important and which ones are not. For service to work, we must not just accept the idea of equality; we must accept it in our hearts and act on it in our lives.

As with charity, equality begins at home. It is not simply about other people; it is also about ourselves – we have to believe we are equal to others as well as seeing others as equal to ourselves. Discouragement threatens our sense of equality, so it is crucial to work on encouraging ourselves and others to achieve true, equal service. The more people feel discouraged, the less they believe in their equality with others and their ability to contribute. The more people are encouraged, the more they will accept that they can contribute to others, and be able to serve in good heart.

Equality is not about only doing something if it will be reciprocated; it is as much to do with attitudes as deeds. It means not being determined by others and defined in relation to them, but rather that our characteristics and skills are given equal value. This does not mean denying that people have strengths and weaknesses, some skills and tasks at which they excel and others at which they do not. For example, when a couple who live together face a task or difficulty it is often tackled not by both partners, but by the partner who is best able or best prepared to do it. There will be other occasions where the other partner will be the right one to carry out what needs to be done. What counts is that both partners do things for each other, and that they trust each other without judgement.

It is not just in practical matters that individuals can encourage each other equally; such encouragement should also apply on a deeper, inner level. For example, even in the most equal partnerships, many men do not wish to show weakness in front of women. They often feel emotionally inhibited, holding on to some outdated concept of male machismo, and will not admit emotional pain when they really need support. This can make it very difficult for a woman to offer help, to 'serve' her friend or partner unselfishly, when it is needed.

In intimate relationships and more formal ones, individuals should strive for equal service, relying on mutual honesty, without either party feeling the need to be something they are not, or to disguise aspects of themselves.

the path to successful service

There are three key features of successful service:

1. taking responsibility It must be your decision to undertake a service for someone else, so it is important that you take responsibility for what you do. You should do this on a task-by-task basis, but you should also take responsibility for what could be called your 'service obligations'.

Always have at the back of your mind what you should be doing for your friends, relatives, family and colleagues.

2. being patient   Always be patient when you are serving someone. Remember that the goal of service is to benefit the other person, not yourself. If the person you are serving irritates you or behaves in a displeasing way, do not take it as an indication of disrespect and reproach them for it, either in your heart or verbally. In doing so, you are unconsciously striving for superiority over them and are not being true to the ideal of service. As we have discussed many times in this book, feeling superior to another person is a negative and essentially false way of asserting your self-belief.

3. not judging   Related to the point we have just discussed is the importance of putting judgement aside. Despite our good intentions, we all have a strong interest in the faults of our fellow human beings; we are all too quick to judge. But we cannot serve people in good faith if, within ourselves, we are criticizing them.

spiritual service

For many people, the highest form of service is the worship of God. As an example of perfect, spiritual service, let us end this chapter with the story of Brother Lawrence, a devout monk who lived in the seventeenth century. Born of humble parents, he served first as a soldier, then a footman in a great French family. At the age of 55, he entered the Carmelite Order in Paris as a lay brother. His responsibilities in the monastery were in the kitchen, where he performed all sorts of menial tasks. But he derived joy from serving his fellow brothers, and from the knowledge that in serving them he was also serving God. He was always cheerful and happy, and even bishops made pilgrimages to visit and learn from this 'most lowly' servant who spent his entire life in joy and happiness. Brother Lawrence was happy because he did everything in a spirit of service, seeing no distinction between menial service and spiritual devotion:

The time of business does not with me differ from the time of prayer; and in the noise and clutter of my kitchen, while several persons are at the same time calling for different things, I possess God in as great tranquillity as if I were upon my knees at the Blessed Sacrament.

Brother Lawrence

For those without religious conviction, service can also be a spiritual endeavour. Many may sense as they serve others, with honesty of thought and humility of heart, that they are fulfilling a humanitarian purpose, enriching their own life and the lives of those around them.

---

six steps to successful service

1. encourage both yourself and others
2. believe in your equality and the equality of others
3. accept your strengths and weaknesses and those of others
4. do not seek your service to be reciprocated
5. be responsible, patient and do not judge
6. see service as an important step along your spiritual path

---

7 prayer, contemplation and meditation

Prayer is often defined as the bond linking humankind to the divine, our means of communion with God. Indeed, all the major world religions emphasize that a sense of spirituality can be found through prayer, contemplation or meditation. If we pray to God, we will not only feel the strength of His guidance; we will also feel our faith rejuvenated by the experience, and our belief in the future renewed. Even for those without religious conviction, the practice of prayer, contemplation or meditation – most of what I say applies to all three – is a form of spiritual food; it is balm for the soul, a light for the heart, a spiritual elevation of our innermost being. Prayer contributes to the growth of our spiritual faculties and skills, in particular insight and understanding. The quietness and calmness of contemplation helps us focus our thoughts and feelings on the issues that either trouble or delight us and can help us to see the way forward, unbothered by peripheral problems.

Prayer can best be described as a state of deep reflection; when we pray or meditate, we commune with our own spirit and think deeply on key subjects. We tune in to ourselves and, if we believe in God, to God's power and mercy. We become detached from ourselves and see with our second sight, our inner eye, untroubled by our first sight, which is preoccupied with the material world. Prayer turns our attention away from ourselves and the material world to the greater issues of the spirit; in so doing, it also renews our spiritual powers and strengthens our self-belief. It is the only means by which we can find genuine satisfaction in life and inner peace.

> *. . . More things are wrought by prayer*
> *Than this world dreams of.*
>
> Alfred, Lord Tennyson

why pray?

We can pray for people – for ourselves or for those we love – our partner, our parents, our children, friends and relations. We can pray for those we have lost or for humanity at large.

We can pray for physical healing, for spiritual growth and well-being. We can ask for virtues and powers, such as humility, patience, detachment, steadfastness, understanding, love and faith. We can ask for guidance and support, strength in times of stress and difficulty, and for peace, both inner peace and peace in the world.

Or we can meditate with less tangible thoughts in order to connect with our spiritual selves.

There are many reasons to pray or meditate – each person will have their own motivation – but there are some goals that most of us will have in common. Most of us pray to be better people, to obtain peace both for ourselves and others and to become more spiritual. In prayer and meditation we tend to work to overcome the shortcomings in our character and in the world. We can seek strength to conquer our ego and our lack of self-belief.

At times of contemplation we feel at the same time both more in touch with our inner being and detached from ourselves. We are more in touch as the troubles and distractions of the outside world are put to one side, but at the same time we can examine our inner selves and consciously decide to change what we find. We can use our open frame of mind and consciousness to tune in to our inner selves, use our second sight, and deal with issues that lie buried deep beneath the surface. This can be a particularly good context to deal with problems concerning our self-belief. We all too often deny low self-belief, but at times of prayer, contemplation or meditation, we have to be honest and face the vulnerable core of ourselves.

Meditate profoundly, that the secret of things unseen may be revealed unto you, that you may inhale the sweetness of a spiritual and imperishable fragrance . . .

Bahá'u'lláh

where to pray

You can pray in designated houses of worship, buildings set aside for worship and prayer, such as temples or churches. Here you can either be alone, free from outside disturbance, or pray along with others. Or you can meditate at home – perhaps in a particularly comfortable chair in which you like to relax, or even while you are washing up! Or you can contemplate outside, perhaps in the peace and quiet of the mountains, or in your garden. You can pray anywhere, really, but the most important consideration is that the location is conducive to contemplation and meditation, that it is quiet and relaxing, somewhere you feel comfortable and where you are unlikely to be disturbed for the length of time you wish to pray.

when to pray

Just as there are no hard and fast rules about where to pray, you can also pray at any time. Many people pray at regular times, perhaps in the early morning or in the evening, and/or before they undertake a particular task. If you are a member of a religious community, you will probably pray about particular things on feast days or other holy days. The only guidance on when to pray that I would give is that regular meditation or prayer is more rewarding than the occasional prayer when one feels the need. Prayer is like any other activity; it improves with practice, so 'little but often' is definitely good advice when it comes to developing a routine for prayer that is spiritually fulfilling.

At the same time as it is spiritually rewarding to make prayer or contemplation a regular part of our lives, we should take care not to 'overdo' it. Prayer should never lose its specialness or become a chore – it should always be an uplifting and encouraging experience. But we must also be careful not to misuse prayer to avoid the tasks we must face in our lives, as sincere prayer is not a valid alternative to conscious action.

how to pray

Although prayer and meditations can be uttered out loud, prayers can be produced in any form – spoken, thought or even written. Whichever way you choose to pray, the most important thing is that prayer is undertaken with complete sincerity, and is positive in nature. Ideally, prayers should be offered with gratitude, joy and dedication, with humility, purity and self-detachment. No form of contemplation will have a positive outcome either for the person who is praying, or for what/who they are praying for, if the prayers are spoken or thought without pureness of heart, or if they are uttered out of fear, or out of a sense of duty. It is crucial to adopt the right attitude of mind. The idea of prayer is that you open your soul to peace and openness; you reflect on issues and pray that you may be enlightened in some way. But as no one can speak and reflect at the same time, however you choose to pray, you should always incorporate a time for silence. You should also never prejudge the outcome of prayer, whatever your religious beliefs. Prayer is a way of opening your heart; you can hope for an outcome but you can never expect it.

Just as it is important for our self-belief to develop consistency between word and deed, we should strive for consistency between prayer and action. The two should be regarded as true companions in our spiritual journey – if we desire something through our prayers, we must also strive for it through our actions; otherwise our efforts are only half in earnest and we will not travel far.

what to pray

You can pray using the writings of the holy scriptures or you can devise your own, but this can be a difficult task. You must take care that prayers do not become too egocentric or too often directed at material things. And it is sometimes fruitless to meditate without words or thoughts to direct our contemplations. I find it helpful to contemplate statements or insights to help me live my life how I would wish it to be. You could use the ones I have included here or just use them as a guide to produce your own. The insights that follow should help you guide your prayers towards your aim of developing your self belief; they are in no particular order. You will find insights on other topics in Appendix 2 on pp. 129–32. We have already discussed many of these insights in this book, but you may find it helpful to have them collected together.

insights on self-belief

I am absolutely unique.

I am important for my contemporaries.

I must learn to believe in the future.

I can change myself.

I have undreamt-of powers latent within me.

I can learn to be happy.

I must not overestimate the importance of success and failure.

Courage is faith in myself.

Fear is belief that I cannot cope.

I should make decisions more consciously.

That I make mistakes makes me human.

I must turn major faults into minor ones.

I can decide my feelings and emotions myself.

I should think more independently.

I, like everyone, can learn to love more.

It is never too late but always high time.

It is better to agree on something that is wrong than to fight
for what I think is right.

I should not attach importance to negative things.

I must acknowledge my good qualities.

I should work consciously to achieve inner peace.

The less I believe in myself, the more egocentric I am.

I can overcome egocentrism through self-encouragement.

I should strive to become spontaneous and loving, rather than
impulsive and emotional.

I should use fewer excuses.

I should trust others more and be less suspicious.

I should be ready to adapt myself without conforming.

I should never give up.

I should not let myself be discouraged, nor should I discourage others.

I should strive for purer motives.

getting the balance right

Everything in human society is about achieving a balance between seemingly opposing forces; if balance is not achieved, the consequence is suffering for all. For example, the human population comprises males and females; if one or other of the sexes is suppressed or privileged, all people suffer. Society is also made up of various races; if one race dominates or becomes dominant, again, all people suffer. Our world consists of various cultures; if one culture is disregarded or becomes dominant, all the other cultures suffer. Human society is made up of children, adults and elderly people; if one of these groups is neglected or given preference, the whole of society suffers. Society can unfortunately be divided into rich and poor; if the rich enjoy greater prestige than the poor, this is harmful to all members of society.

Similarly, the individual human being is composed of body, soul and spirit. If we neglect or pamper our bodies, the person as a whole will suffer. We must look after the development of our soul and spirit, otherwise we will not become the person we have the potential to be. We must take care of ourselves in all senses, achieving a balance between our physical and spiritual needs so that we can grow, not just by adding pounds to our body weight, but also in our inner selves.

As we have discovered, to restore the balance of our outer and inner lives we have at our disposal our ability to make conscious decisions. So far in this book we have talked about applying our decision-making abilities within specific contexts, but in this chapter we will be looking at how we can draw on all the practical and spiritual strategies we have covered, such as our capacity for insight, our growing ability to love and our sense of faith, to make a conscious decision about our self-belief. We will do this by considering the following case study. As we analyse it, we will also explore the key examples of balance we should strive for to achieve our maximum personal development.

> Like many other people, when Kate comes home in the evening she usually complains about the amount of work she has to do, about how boring her job is, or about how stupidly her boss or colleagues have been behaving. The next morning she unwillingly drags herself out of bed, sighs and expects her family to have pity on her because of her hard life. She further tries to encourage sympathy from her family by stressing how she has only taken on this terrible burden for their sake. In reality, the family is sick and tired of Kate's constant moaning. As much as they appreciate her unhappiness, annoyance and resentment are starting to take over.

What is Kate's problem? Why is she behaving like this? What does it tell us about her self-belief? If we look at her behaviour in terms of the short-term goals covered in Chapter 1, we may learn something that will help us understand. Perhaps Kate is critical about her boss and her colleagues as a means of hiding her own shortcomings, to disguise her own lack of self-belief. There is little doubt that she is seeking care and attention, particularly the latter, as her persistent moaning is a call for pity and sympathy from her family. Her criticism of her boss and colleagues also indicates she is pursuing a sense of superiority. Perhaps this is because she feels the job she is doing is below her, and she is overcompensating for her own feeling of inferiority. She may also be seeking revenge, either on her employers for some event we do not know about, or on her family; perhaps she genuinely does not feel they appreciate her, either because of her hard work or something else – or both.

Whatever specific goals Kate is working towards, she is definitely overcompensating for some feeling of self-doubt, of low self-belief, and that is what she has to work at, following the techniques we have described in this book. First she must change her attitude – at present she perceives herself as the victim. Everything is just happening to her without her taking any active part. She must seize her capacity for conscious decision-making, she must act rather than react. She must realize that life is only as difficult as we see it and make it, and it is our responsibility to change our life if we do not like the course it is taking.

being positive and realistic

If Kate accepts and acts on her ability to make conscious decisions, she would be taking a step towards being positive; she would feel more in control and more able to shape situations for herself. But being positive means more than feeling that we are in control. It means we approach situations from a positive direction. Being positive does not mean that we do not see what is negative in our lives, or sweep it under the carpet. That would amount to self-delusion. Being positive means remaining aware of negative things, but not being prepared to attach great importance to them. We remain realistic but emphasize the positive. With the aid of our sense of faith and our capacity for insight, we can discern something positive in everything that seems negative. In this way, we feel less drained by difficulties, and experience a greater sense of freedom.

Kate sees little that is positive in her work and it is clear that her perspective needs to change unless she takes positive action towards finding different work. There are probably more than a couple of aspects to her work that she could view positively. She should make a conscious decision to see not only her work but also her colleagues and her boss in a more positive light. She should think about why she works and what she does to make a positive contribution to the company. She could think of a positive thing to do at work each day to make her want to get up in the morning. She could also ask her family to help her not to complain so much and report so many negative things by agreeing some sort of brief sign with them (rotating a thumbs-down gesture into a thumbs-up?) that they should give as soon as they notice she is slipping back into a negative mode. Not just Kate herself, but the whole family would be happier as a result. All this will not make the negative aspects of Kate's job go away, but will at least help her evaluate her situation with a more balanced perspective. From there she can make a conscious decision about what path to follow to achieve a positive outcome.

work and play

Another part of Kate's problem is the overwhelming role that work plays in her life. She thinks about it from when she gets up to when she goes to bed and since her thoughts on her work are so overwhelmingly negative, they sour her day and her family's too. Her work is more important to her than her family, let alone any other leisure pursuit. Unfortunately, her situation is not atypical. Many families suffer because one member of the family pays excessive attention to his or her work, depriving the family of his or her company. It is sometimes inevitable that work is given first priority, but it should only be for a limited time; if it becomes a permanent state of affairs, the happiness of the entire family is seriously compromised. If the overemphasis on work continues, it may suggest that the individual is motivated too much by standards of personal success and the prestige he or she perceives within society. Kate and those like her need to treat their work as just one aspect of life. If we can start to work to live rather than live to work, and explore leisure activities to balance the time we spend working, we will not only benefit personally, but those who live with us will benefit too. Together, we can spend time doing things we had had hitherto missed out on.

self and society

Another aspect of Kate's problem is that her attention is focused exclusively on herself. She sees herself as an individual in opposition to her family rather than accepting her role as a family member: contributing to it and being supported by it during personally difficult times.

As we have discussed, successful social living of all kinds, from partnerships to families to communities, relies on the equality of all the individuals involved. At the same time, neither the needs of the individual nor those of the community should dominate. Individuals must strike a balance between their own needs and those of the people around them.

Achieving a balance between self and society also extends to balancing family and community life. A family benefits when the relationships within it are successful and balanced, but we also need to look beyond these to the larger community. It is extremely important to strike a balance between family life and life in common with others; with friends, acquaintances, relatives and the community at large. Without balancing self-responsibility and our shared responsibility for society we fail to do justice to our common identity as human beings. If responsibility for others, for the wider community, is not developed it can lead to a sense of self-satisfaction or even self-righteousness. Whilst ensuring we adapt rather than conform (see pp. 71–2), we should interact with others, or else we will not flourish but will become lonely and impoverished. Everyone needs interaction with others, not only because we can learn from them but because we also give them the chance to learn from us. But that is not all. If we develop a sense of community from pure motives and the right attitude, it feeds the spirit: it teaches not only faith in oneself, but also love for others, for the community and for the whole of humankind.

As well as balancing self and society, Kate has to achieve balance within herself, to attain a sense of inner peace, which a journey along the path of spiritualization will bring. If Kate can achieve the major goal of living at peace with herself, she can also contribute to lessening other people's feelings of unhappiness and fear and help them to become less self-centred and nervous.

the material and the spiritual

In this book, you will have noticed how much of what we have been exploring in our attempt to develop self-belief has involved balancing the material, practical aspects of life with the spiritual sides of our being – balancing the needs of the body, soul and spirit. Much as the material aspects of life are important for us as we pursue our everyday lives, we need the spiritual too in order to find solutions to the problems we face. Fortunately, it is less widely thought today that the practical – the world of facts and science – and the spiritual must be kept separate. More and more people, even leading scientists, are including religion and spirituality in their considerations. People are, after all, spiritual beings, whatever their beliefs, and many people now recognize the merits of a 'spiritual principle', or what for some has long been termed 'God'.

moderation in all things

This book has attempted to show how, through a combination of practical and spiritual principles, by getting to know ourselves better both as individuals and social beings, we can establish and nurture our sense of self-belief. As this last chapter has established, the key to success is balance, not to let any one aspect of our lives take over to upset our natural equilibrium. As we discussed in Chapter 1, we need to take a holistic view, neither neglecting or overemphasizing any aspect of ourselves. If we achieve moderation in all things, we should achieve outer and inner peace.

Water does not occupy more space than it really needs. Hence, it is like moderation.

Confucius

appendix one

interpretation of goals

Here is my interpretation of the goals the individuals we discussed on p. 16 are pursuing. How do my thoughts compare with yours?

Karen's goal is care and attention (goal 2). Although probably unconsciously, she blushes to get attention.

This woman considers housework as inferior to her husband's work. By making him take on some typical household chores, she obtains a feeling of superiority (goal 3) over him.

We do not know the circumstances of James' change of attitude towards his wife's sexual needs a few months ago. It could be that he has become preoccupied with the difference in their ages and is afraid that he will not always be able to satisfy her (goal 1). Or perhaps his desire for sex is less strong than hers and he is worried that she will regard him as inferior, as not a 'real man' (goal 3). Or maybe he is trying to 'punish' her for something else in their partnership where he feels she does not always fulfil his needs (goal 4). Or it could be goal 5, perhaps in connection with something at work that we do not know about. It may even be that all five goals are involved, but more often than not there is one goal that predominates.

It is very likely that Tom has the impression that his father does not love him, because of the amount of criticism he receives and because his rather is always pushing him to learn and achieve more. Tom is punishing his father for this (goal 4). He is not always conscious of this, but does have the feeling that his father is less interested in Tom than in himself.

appendix two

insights on society

I am responsible both for myself and for society.
A sense of community is faith in my fellow human beings.
Social equality for all is one of the main tasks facing us today.
We should all encourage one another.
We should strive to serve others.
We should lessen our interest in other people's faults.
We should not seek to be in the right.
Justifying oneself is often harmful.
We should believe in society.
We should not cut ourselves off from others.
We should strike a balance between love and justice.
We should love others instead of criticizing them.
Constructive criticism is helpful.
To win respect is more important than to win popularity.
Courtesy is one of the most important virtues for community
    life.

insights on life

Optimism is worth striving for.
It is often more important to recognize goals than to look for
    reasons.
Facts count less than what I make of them.
Everyone has the right to a sense of belonging.
Everyone has faults in their life style.
I need belief in perfection and the courage to be imperfect.

I know more than I understand.

I must first learn from the past, then forget it.

Through greater awareness our motives become purer.

To act is more important than to react.

I should express myself more precisely.

I should become more aware of my inner senses.

I should abandon all forms of prejudice.

Attitudes are easier to change than emotions.

To love what one does is more important than to do what one
loves.

I should develop more patience.

We should lessen our readiness for conflict.

'Both–and' is more important than the old 'either–or'
approach.

We should always learn to try to see the whole.

I should not demand, but request, conversation.

Fear is belief in something negative.

Joyfulness can be learned.

What matters is balance.

The negative is merely absence of the positive.

Complaining gets us nowhere.

I should test the value of new things, not be afraid of them.

It is more important to do what is right than to seek success.

We should not exalt ourselves above others.

We should not give other people unfair advantages.

I should be grateful.

I should be tolerant.

I should not put others down.

I should practise moderation rather than excess.

I should make good use of my free time.

We should become peaceful instead of aggressive.

We should welcome every task we are confronted with and
not regard it as 'difficult'.

Empathy is better than pity.

Initiative is a sign of courage.

Look for the root cause behind the obvious problem.

We should do something good every day.

A radiant person makes others happy.

Enthusiasm is contagious.

Caution is always appropriate, fear never.

Life is a process of overcoming.

If we are embarking on a new plan of action, we must constantly have its outcome in mind.

It is all right to lose a battle, but one must not lose the war.

Only a courageous person can have humility without being humiliated.

insights on spirituality

I should refine my spiritual faculties.

I need to find a balance between body, soul and spirit.

Spiritualization is the purpose of life.

Insight is more than knowledge.

Faith is more than hope.

Faith is the only way to achieve certainty.

We should believe in life in itself and in our own life.

We can learn to have faith by investing faith.

We grow not by adding pounds to our body weight, but by developing spiritually.

We should make our eyes see more positively.

Inner resignation helps no one.

Spirituality is the opposite of egocentrism.

We should prefer spiritual possessions to material ones.

We are spiritual beings.

The intellect, the heart and the spirit are all involved in faith.

I must pray for my parents, my family, my friends and my enemies as well as myself.

Love all humanity and promote the well-being of humankind.

guide for a fulfilling life

Let thoughts be translated into deeds.

Strive to make others happy and to support them.

Keep silent about others' faults and help them.

Patiently endure resistance and insults.

Never speak unkindly of others.

Try not to cause other people worry.

Strive to be kind to everyone.

Look to the good in everything.

Be hospitable.

Be courteous.

Be humble.

Do not be egocentric.

Do not argue.

Be tolerant.

Encourage others.

Be just.

Perceive through both mind and heart.

Lay prejudice aside.

Strive for physical and spiritual purity.

Put the spiritual world above the material.

Act with caution and wisdom.

Be dutiful in work and family life.

Be honest.

Be selfless.

Show love by means of deeds and not by words alone.

Pay attention to the small and weak.

Avoid violence and repression.

Be optimistic about the future of all that is good, true and beautiful.

Recognize unity in diversity and diversity in unity.